MILLENNIAL REBOOT

MILLENNIAL REBOOT

Our Generation's Playbook for Professional Growth

KATE ATHMER AND ROB JOHNSON

LIONCREST
PUBLISHING

MILLENNIAL REBOOT: OUR GENERATION'S
PLAYBOOK FOR PROFESSIONAL GROWTH

Kate Athmer & Rob Johnson

ISBN   978-1-61961-538-0 *Paperback*

978-1-61961-539-7 *Ebook*

To our friends and fellow Millennials.

CONTENTS

INTRODUCTION 11

PART I: GET IT TOGETHER
1. WHAT YOU NEED TO KNOW (OR SHOULD
   ALREADY KNOW AND PRACTICE) 25
2. UNDERSTANDING BASIC LEADERSHIP STYLES............. 81

PART II: HOW TO NAVIGATE LEADERSHIP STYLES
3. MANAGING UP.................................... 101
4. IDEA ADVANCEMENT................................ 121
5. CAREER ADVANCEMENT 135

PART III: HOW TO LEVEL UP
6. ALWAYS BE LEARNING............................. 163
7. SUSTAINING SUCCESS 183

CONCLUSION 199
ADDITIONAL RESOURCES 203
ACKNOWLEDGMENTS 205
ABOUT THE AUTHORS 207

· ·

INTRODUCTION

· ·

"MILLENNIALS."

Yes, we despise this label, too. How did we get to the point
where the largest generation in American history can be
typecast as one singular entity with a branding problem?

Some of us remember the struggles paired with a high-
pitched dial-up sound, many are lamenting that we aren't
living off the once-promised fortunes of our Beanie Baby
collection, and all of us have spent a significant part of our
lives with instant access to almost any information. Inar-
guably, those of us born from the early 1980s to around
2000 have witnessed the largest shift in human communication in history.

So, who exactly are "we," the authors, and why should you listen to us?

In addition to our nine-to-five jobs, we've also taken on side gigs that have included coaching our peers—both in work and in life—and founded GreenLit Consulting, which provides hands-on small business and personal brand consulting.

Our success has been the result of whining less and working harder and smarter, but also being graced with some amazing people who have helped us along the way. Their help gave us a huge advantage when it came to accelerating our careers, and we want to do the same for you.

In other words, we get it.

Let's look at a few stereotypes we're up against.

1. MILLENNIALS ARE LAZY

While interviewing executives for this book, we certainly heard many unflattering stories about the Millennial work ethic, or should we say, "perceived" work ethic. Many will throw stats out, such as the Addison Group poll that stated that "40 percent of Millennials expect a promotion every one to two years." Okay, well, if that's true, doesn't it also mean that more than half of this generation expects hard work to earn us a promotion? Where's *that* sensationalized headline in the news cycle?

It's no secret that Millennials perceive work ethic much differently than past generations do. Being chained to one desk for forty hours a week doesn't make a lot of sense when we could just as easily and efficiently reply to emails, prepare a presentation, or review a pitch from any location with a solid Wi-Fi connection. Yes, there are certainly the lazy and unmotivated, as is the case with any group, but we're going to focus on the efficiently awesome. We would bet that if you're reading this, you fit in the latter.

2. MILLENNIALS HAVE A SENSE OF ENTITLEMENT

We have access to and can apply for virtually any job in any part of the world. So, it's fair to assume a dream career that aligns closely with our passionate interests is attainable sooner rather than later, when we've "paid our dues." Much of that belief, though, stems from having worked in a series of underpaid positions related to our education and experience level. Regardless, the good news is that the perception of being entitled can be controlled by one's actions, which we'll talk about later in the book.

3. MILLENNIALS ARE SERIAL JOB-HOPPERS

Job-hopping early in a career is as common today as it was in the 1980s according to the United States Bureau of Labor Statistics. Early in anyone's career, there is less to tie us down and prevent us from taking the risks and advantages of a higher salary, advanced position, or just a better fit in the company culture.

4. MILLENNIALS WANT A TROPHY FOR EVERYTHING

Research from Forbes, PricewaterhouseCoopers, and Deloitte shows that we aren't looking for a "trophy" but for a solid feedback system with our managers that goes beyond the traditional annual review. In the coming chapters, you'll learn how to ask for more detailed, ongoing feedback without coming across as needy.

Between these and countless other negative stereotypes as well as our twenty-four-hour, always-on, camera-everywhere society, no wonder there's an inflated perception of how awful we are.

Is this book going to prove that all these stereotypes are wrong? No. There are some things we totally suck at, and plenty of things we were just never taught. But we do have a tremendous gift in that we are all Digital Natives, familiar with technology from an early age. We can Google, YouTube, or creatively think our way out of many situations better than any other stereotyped generation this world has produced.

We just need a reboot, and it starts with solving our communication problem.

Learning how to communicate value without undermining your managers is one of the key components to your success. What might seem like a no-brainer to you will most likely be foreign or out of context to your higher-ups.

It's why our generation often feels stuck at their job, undervalued, and unheard. Millennials spent their formative years feasting on an all-you-can-eat buffet of Facebook, Amazon, and Netflix while superiors enjoyed an entrée of NBC and side dishes of CBS and ABC. When we get into a large corporation and see what's on the menu, we can easily lose our appetites.

Digital Natives have no idea why this awesome technology we've grown so accustomed to using isn't being used to its full potential—why no one else seems to understand how much *better* everything could be.

A Deloitte 2016 Millennial survey found that only 28 percent of Millennials believe their employers are taking full advantage of their skills. Combine that with a recent Gallup poll in which a clear majority of Millennials admitted to not being engaged at the office, and it's completely understandable why the perception is that not much work is getting done by people under the age of thirty-five.

"Okay," people have probably said to you, "If you don't like the way the corporate world treats you, then your best bet is to become an entrepreneur." Our social media feeds are filled with stories like "*Couple quit midlevel corporate jobs to travel the world and start their own business!*"

That's all well and good, but not everyone has the capability—financially, mentally, or otherwise—to be running their own business before they're thirty.

Not to mention, major companies like GE, IBM, and Proctor & Gamble aren't going away anytime soon, and somebody has to run them. Contrary to the statistics and newspaper headlines all screaming about the "Me, Me, Me Generation," there are those of us who are willing and ready to put the time in, suck it up, and do the hard work.

If you want to go into business for yourself, awesome. However, you'd be better served spending someone else's money before spending your own. Go to a company and learn. Build your skill set. Figure out what you're good at and where you need to improve. Network and build relationships. Find mentors. Make your mistakes while the stakes are low, not when they're high.

While you're gaining experience, and earning credibility, use this book as your survival guide.

It doesn't matter if you're stuck in a cubicle or ruling the world from a corner office. You're going to have to figure out the following:

- ⏻ Why you can't get along with a particular person at work
- ⏻ How to properly manage up and positively engage the worst boss/client ever
- ⏻ Why it's a good idea to keep a blazer in your office at all times
- ⏻ How to bring fresh ideas to a stale corporate framework
- ⏻ How to effectively handle uncomfortable conversations regarding the larger paycheck you desire
- ⏻ Who to avoid if you want to advance your career

If you want someone to tell you how amazingly perfect and awesome you are, and how *lucky* any company would be to have you, call your mom. If you want straightforward, been-there-done-that words of wisdom, then stay tuned. Because we get it. We've tasted the sweetness of success and had to swallow some bitter failures along the way.

We know what most of corporate America thinks of our generation and vice versa. As you can probably already guess, it isn't always pretty. What we've learned, sometimes the hard way, is that it will benefit you tremendously to be less of a Millennial asshole and instead learn how to present new ideas and new technologies in very relatable ways. Showing people up doesn't advance your career; bringing people with you and growing together does.

Being a Millennial in today's working world can be extremely frustrating and make you feel as if you're beating your head against a wall. It's easy to become complacent and convinced nothing will ever change.

It will. We promise. But it's going to take some finesse and patience on your part.

Our generation must always remain cognizant that the way we choose to communicate still needs to hold respect for established corporate culture and processes. We can't go in guns blazing, wanting to change everything all at once, but a happy medium does exist. There are tools you can learn to more effectively forward your perspectives and ideas within the framework of existing structures.

In other words, become proficient at turning your ideas into actions. As creator of the *Dilbert* comic strip Scott Adams said in his book *How to Fail at Almost Everything and Still Win Big: Kind of the Story of My Life*, "The market rewards execution, not ideas."

When Rob was a freshman in college, he got a glimpse at how business played a role in professional sports when his professor became involved in a broadcast of the NFL's Hall of Fame game.

Interest piqued, he set his sights on an internship with the Eagles, his hometown team.

So, he asked around. "Do you know anybody at the Eagles?" He applied online. Both got him nowhere. By the time his junior year rolled around, his staple introduction became "Hi, I'm Rob; do you know anybody who works with the Philadelphia Eagles?"

Eventually, he found someone who knew someone else, and through those connections he scored an internship.

By senior year, he figured out his dream job: senior marketing executive in the NFL. Every job description included a preference for MBAs. As a frugal college student, it dawned on him that his rowing experience might be enough to cinch a job as a graduate assistant coach. If he did, chances were good that whatever school hired him would also offer discounted tuition to employees. Savvy research and networking led him to Jacksonville University. While pursuing a graduate degree, he wanted to add an internship with the Jacksonville Jaguars to his resume.

Again, he asked around. Nothing. He applied to internships. Nothing. Then one day, he was in the cafeteria and saw a job posting calling for applications to drive the Jaguars' ice-cream truck.

Without flinching, he applied. On the day of the interview, he showed up with a twenty-page business plan on how he was going to make this ice-cream truck the best thing that Northeast Florida had ever seen.

"Stop," the interviewers said. "We can't have you driving this truck. We have a bigger job in mind, which is a paid internship with the marketing and special events department. Come back next week and interview."

So he did, and six months into his internship he was hired for a full-time job.

Being overprepared worked.

The moral to this story? There are no shortcuts to hard work and relationships if you want to turn your ideas into actions.

HOW DO YOU KNOW THIS BOOK IS FOR YOU?

Consider which of the following describe you:

- ⏻ It doesn't bother me to be called a "Millennial."
- ⏻ I don't need to hide any part of my online presence from Grandma.
- ⏻ I can articulate my personal brand in less than fifteen seconds.
- ⏻ There are plenty of opportunities for advancement in my company.
- ⏻ I feel zero frustration about my current role and compensation.
- ⏻ I'm confident in my ability to navigate tough scenarios and come out on top.
- ⏻ I negotiate effectively for what I want.
- ⏻ I have plenty of workplace relationships that I can leverage as needed.
- ⏻ I participate in workplace politics—in a good way.
- ⏻ I advocate for my peers.
- ⏻ I have hobbies and passions outside my job other than TV.
- ⏻ I participate in plenty of responsible social interaction.

If all of those statements are true for you, you probably don't need this book. Gift it to a friend, then shoot us a note at protips@millennialreboot.com or tweet @RebootBook with some of your best advice.

If only a few of those statements are true for you, then great—you're probably doing okay for yourself but looking for a little extra oomph. Some of this might seem basic to you; just grab a PSL (pumpkin-spice latte) and read on for the good stuff.

However, if only a few of those are true on a good day, it's time for a reboot.

PART I

—

GET IT TOGETHER

CHAPTER 1

· ·

WHAT YOU NEED TO KNOW

· ·

(OR SHOULD ALREADY KNOW AND PRACTICE)

PEOPLE HAVE always used their connections to get a job.

Now, thirty or forty years ago, that might have meant working alongside Uncle John at his neighborhood grocery store. Maybe it wasn't a dream job, but hey, the ink was barely dry on their college degree, it was real-world experience, and it made their resume look meaty.

Job leads were often limited to classified ads in the local paper or the hot tip from your dad's accountant's brother. Also, people had to rely on skills they already had, limiting them to apply for jobs within those skill sets. "Putting in your time" was a requirement for advancement because you had to learn everything on the job. In today's world, you can learn things in your spare time through online resources, which often translates into an accelerated career track.

Yeah, you might be thinking, *that's why networking is a waste of time.*

Which is exactly what we figured you'd say.

Yes, you can see every job posted in the world in one place— but remember, so can everyone else.

Technology has guaranteed there'll be more competition, more likelihood that your resume is one of one thousand being delivered to a black hole of nameless, soulless, automated collection. It's also fostered the idea that you shouldn't waste your time applying for a position that doesn't qualify as your dream job. According to the article "How the American Workforce is Changing" by workintelligent.ly, there are 41 percent more people over the age of fifty-five in the workplace today than there were in 2001. People aren't retiring as early as they did in previous generations, which means there are fewer senior positions to advance into.

Because resources were so limited in the past, people were more willing to put their time in, pay their dues. Getting your dream job right out of college? Please. Dream jobs were a reward for shedding vast amounts of blood, sweat, and tears for twenty-five years. Even the idea of a dream job was different back then: it mostly meant a stable job and a pension, and it had little to do with finding something "fulfilling." It was expected that you had to rely on your connections, relationships, and introductions to steadily work your way into more senior roles.

We've lost sight of that, falling under the misguided belief that technology ensures we'll always make the right connections with the right people at the right time.

It's the professional equivalent to the mentality surrounding your so-called soul mate: Until the perfect job comes along, we're content to swipe left. After all, there are limitless possibilities out there! The world is at our fingertips! Why settle?

So, you keep waiting for The One.

Waiting...and waiting...and waiting.

In Austin Kleon's book *Steal Like an Artist: 10 Things Nobody Told You About Being Creative*, he says that nothing is more paralyzing than the idea of limitless possibilities.

In other words, you need to stop waiting for a "perfect" job to appear at your door like a knight in shining armor. Limitless opportunities don't always guarantee bigger and better. Dr. Seuss wrote his best-selling book, *Green Eggs and Ham*, on a fifty-dollar bet from his publisher that he couldn't write a book with fifty words or less.

Constraints aren't always a bad thing. When it comes to finding the perfect job, be open to the idea that it might not be a 100 percent match of what you're looking for. But dig a little deeper. Objectively weigh whether it will sharpen and widen your skill set, and figure out how you might be able to use it as leverage for upward mobility in your career.

If you want to be a world-famous writer, don't limit yourself to applying at the *New York Times*. Find smaller media outlets that would benefit from someone who is willing to work across multiple departments. In doing so, you fatten your resume, gain valuable hands-on experience, and come ready for the next opportunity armed with a portfolio stuffed with bylines.

COMMON CHALLENGE AREAS
DON'T BE A DICK

You're most likely very aware that you are now surrounded by many, many people with many, many different approaches to workplace roles and career-advancement paths.

How to handle them is simple: Don't be a dick.

You can apply that to any person you encounter: janitors, admins, coworkers, middle management, the C-suite. Regardless of how complicated and difficult the other person might be, acting like a dick is **always** the wrong thing to do.

You've got to remember and respect the fact that everyone is coming to the office with his or her own work philosophies that have been influenced by a variety of factors:

- ⏻ **Generations**
- ⏻ **Industries**
- ⏻ **Geographic regions**
- ⏻ **Expectations**

You might not think you share the same values as your boss, who has six grandchildren, held the same job for forty years, and goes to church every Sunday, Tuesday, and Thursday. You may feel that you have absolutely nothing in common with this person and have no way of relating to her.

Guess what? You're wrong!

You can still say, "Just like your grandchildren are really important to you, my friends are really important to me." In that context, you're able to frame any conversation to demonstrate that you not only value where she is coming from but empathize with it as well.

It also prevents you from seeming disinterested and unsociable.

Still not sure what to talk about with your office mates? Since neither of us watch a lot of prime-time television, we subscribe to *The Skimm*, a daily e-newsletter that breaks down trending topics into bite-sized pieces just ICYMI (in case you missed it). That way, when Dave shows up at the watercooler to talk about what GOP lawmakers are freaking out about this time around, you can be armed with just enough information to engage in the conversation, even if you have little interest in politics. Not only does it give insight into what makes Dave tick; it shows you're at least interested enough to hear what he has to say.

Remember, people will develop perceptions of you based on your actions. Even if you're not being a jerk, it's easy to look like one when you're not mindful about certain things.

TECHNOLOGY GAPS

As it pertains to Millennials and previous generations, technology is almost always a case of "us versus them." Our careers have basically been built around the navigation of those waters, tasked with putting technology in terms that people of all experiences can warm to, or see the value in, even if they're not chomping at the bit to buy in.

We experienced this in our personal lives when we started shopping for a new car. The first salesman we countered insisted that he communicate with us via phone even after we indicated a preference for email.

He continued to press, refused to budge, so we moved on.

After shopping around, we received a note from a salesperson who said, "I see that you prefer to begin the conversation via email before you come in and look at the car. I respect that. Here are some options that we have right now."

We immediately warmed to her. Why? Because we felt heard, respected, and valued.

It's important to incorporate those same ideals into your interactions with colleagues at work. People don't respond well to being forced to communicate in a way that is uncomfortable to them, especially from someone younger.

When that happens, don't try to shove your preferred vehicle down their throats. Instead, introduce it slowly. Do some due diligence on how this more efficient method would benefit them, not just you, and then prove it with an appropriately timed, tangible example.

Often, there is probably a better way of doing things than the antiquated systems being employed at work. Don't be afraid to share them. Just be respectful of the fact that the person you're dealing with might not be aware of the latest and greatest technology or comfortable using it. If they shoot it down now, **resist the urge to oversell,** which will create a polarizing win-lose situation. Instead, **ask questions** and **listen** to gain understanding of their reason for resistance. If it's still contentious, shelve it and wait for another opportunity to revisit the idea later.

THE "TRADITIONAL" OFFICE HOURS

Millennials have grown so accustomed to running around with a super computer in our pocket that we forget it's still a relatively new technology. It's easy to take for granted the fact that we can work from virtually anywhere. You no longer must remain tethered to your cubicle to be productive at work.

However, most traditional corporate frameworks still equate the amount of work you do with the amount of time spent in the office. While previous generations place value on years of experience, Millennials place value on hours of experience.

Want to know how to bridge the gap?

Get creative.

If you're expected to be at work from 9:00 a.m. to 5:00 p.m., but your work is done at 3:00 p.m., don't spend two hours mindlessly surfing the Internet or complaining about how stupid it is that you have to just sit there doing nothing.

Yes, it's annoying, but use that time as an opportunity to do something productive. Ask your boss if you can lend a hand on a project another team is working on. Go to another department and volunteer your services as needed. Build a plan that will help increase web traffic.

Get involved, and don't limit yourself to the task at hand. Use your multitasking and digital wizardry to gain additional experience wherever and whenever you can. By doing so, you not only beef up your resume, but you demonstrate leadership skills by making productive use of your time. That's something the higher-ups will take notice of, and slowly the trust door to more flexible hours will start to swing open.

DRESS CODE

Dress for the job you want.

Seriously, it's that simple.

Forget about all those inspirational quotations pinned to your Pinterest board. In the real world, what's on the outside does count. The way that people in the organization perceive you is directly impacted by what you're wearing. Like we said in the introduction, it probably matters even more than the content of what you are saying. Like it or not, people will—and do—judge you based on appearance.

We knew of an engineer who wore a T-shirt and jeans to work all the time. He had no reason to dress up. He was never in front of clients. But one day he had a funeral to attend and came to work wearing a suit. On that day, the CEO who had never acknowledged him before said hello.

Why?

Because the CEO thought this guy was someone worth communicating with.

After that, the engineer went out and bought a wardrobe of more work-appropriate apparel. Thus, senior executives talked to him in the hallways more and engaged him in the lunch room. All because he made a simple change in what he put on in the morning.

So, before you even start a job, do some research and find out how you're expected to dress. Even better, make note of what the senior executives are wearing and tailor your wardrobe accordingly.

Honestly, it's just plain stupid if you don't.

COMMUNICATION

While Millennials might be really good at responding digitally, we tend to suck at engaging people on the phone. This is because we've been raised on a steady diet of texting, instant messaging, and emailing. Not only do we find it to be far more efficient than a phone call, but it can also cover our butts if something goes terribly wrong.

But text-only communication doesn't always fly.

Plain and simple: if your boss would rather speak on the

phone, **then get on the phone**.

It's important to know how the person on the other end prefers to communicate. Once you do, make sure you mirror his or her format and tone.

If the senior vice president emails you a one-liner, don't respond with nine flowery paragraphs accented with super-cute emojis. In fact, the only way to successfully communicate with senior executives today is to be a lean communicator. We recommend Joseph McCormack's book *Brief: Make a Bigger Impact by Saying Less* for a deeper look at mastering this strategy.

On the flip side, if your ad rep is prone to cheerleader-esque emails, don't be curt with your replies. You can still be brief, but keep some personality in it.

Early in his career, Rob would often have colleagues coming up to him with concerned looks on their faces.

"Hey man, what was up with your email?" they would say. "Are you mad or something?"

At first he was taken aback. What in the world were they talking about? His messages were efficiently to the point and cordial.

He quickly learned the value of including the occasional exclamation point or smiley face to convey a friendlier tone. It's what this group needed to feel at ease.

Another example includes Kate and her boss, who one day gave her the following instructions: "Email the client and say, in all caps, NEVER DELETE SHIT and then put a smiley face after it."

That kind of message worked because they had a relationship with the client that was good enough to be able to call them out on something serious, but to do so in a way that was still lighthearted and disarming.

The point is that it is imperative to know your audience and who you're communicating with. You can foster a more productive relationship with people by adapting to their style rather than refusing to budge.

TMI IS B-A-D

Today's world is powered by a bizarre, insatiable need for overshare.

While that might have worked well for the Kardashians, it most likely will do nothing to propel your own career.

There's nothing wrong with friendly conversation about

what you did over the weekend.

But instead of "I got hammered on a boat. Thank god for dry shampoo this morning!" you'd be better off saying: "We watched the football game and caught up with old friends."

(Dry shampoo is a wonderful thing, and Kate is grateful for the hours it's given her back. But do not ever announce to your coworkers that you didn't shower that day. That, and getting tanked, is TMI—too much information.)

You should be able to evaluate how your answer is going to impact your relationship with the person you're talking to, but more importantly, how it will impact your perceived value as an employee. Steer the conversation to something more interesting than the weather, but to a topic that won't likely give you a bad rep.

Apply the same principles to your social media presence. Always be careful not to post inappropriate photos or commentary.

So, what's inappropriate?

Anything you wouldn't show or say to your grandma at church.

Along those same lines, it's not exactly a genius move to be bitching about the company on Twitter or putting a coworker on blast on Facebook. Also, be careful of celebrating an internal win that hasn't yet been designated as public information.

You never know who is watching.

WHY EVERYONE THINKS MILLENNIALS ARE A PAIN IN THE ASS TO WORK WITH

Okay, let's just clear that up right now, because regardless of what you read in the media, not *everyone* thinks this way.

"Far too much emphasis is given to negative aspects of workers from younger generations," says Silicon Valley executive Brandon O'Connor. "I have two team members in this age group who are absolutely fantastic and hard workers. They want to be challenged and have a voice in decisions and how they can improve processes, and I think it's incredible. There are many big strengths that can be leveraged, and every person has unique talents to bring to the table. As leaders, we should ask ourselves how we can do a better job cultivating those abilities."

Yes, much has been written about how difficult it is to manage Millennials. To be fair, some of it is true. Every generation has its own bushel of bad apples, and ours isn't excluded. But it's been our experience that most of the problem stems from communication issues, many of which we just went over.

Unfortunately, compounding our problem is the fact that technology has changed exponentially over the past three decades, probably more so than any other time in history. There's a lack of constructive information and guidance on how to use our skills as Digital Natives to navigate and advance in the traditional office environment.

We get frustrated at work and then become bored. Change comes too slowly, and when it finally does, something bigger and better has already come along.

But while you might understand the technology, it does not mean you understand the **role** of technology in an organization.

Appreciate how fast everything is moving and that you're working with people who might not be able to make that shift as quickly as you can. It's something you need to continuously remind yourself of. Everything that you see in real time might not necessarily be what your bosses are seeing.

It can get annoying and frustrating, but remember: Don't be a dick.

Instead of getting upset that your client wants to use a Word document to beef up an outline, ask if she'd be interested in seeing how a Google doc can more efficiently foster communication and collaboration. Then, offer to give her a quick tutorial to demonstrate how it would work.

Also, in any given situation, try using the word *and* rather than *but*. It's a subtle change that avoids shutting a person down while still expressing your concern or boundary:

- ⏻ "That's a great idea, *but* I'm not sure who could execute it this week given our other priorities."
- ⏻ "That's a great idea, *and* I'm not sure who could execute it this week given our other priorities."

In doing so, you receive the idea in a respectful way that expresses your concerns without shutting the other person down.

PROFESSIONAL BASICS
PERFECT YOUR PERSONAL ELEVATOR PITCH

When you meet anyone anywhere, not just in an elevator, you should be able to represent yourself in fifteen seconds. Here are some guidelines:

1. State your name and title. There's no need for "Hi, I'm…" It will make you sound more confident.

2. Mention one to two things your job entails that you are proud of.

3. If you are speaking with a higher-up, provide one to two key strengths you bring to your workplace. (It's ideal if these strengths came from feedback from a trusted advisor.)

4. Once you've nailed your personal elevator pitch, practice saying it out loud until it easily rolls off the tongue. It should become so natural that you can spit it out even when you're on an elevator with your favorite movie star/a sports hero/a really intimidating CEO.

It's a good idea to have a couple variations of these for different situations. For example, Kate will switch between highlighting her full-time job, featuring her consulting work, and mentioning her work as an author.

NAILING THE ART OF NETWORKING

Back in the day, networking entailed an endless stream of phone calls and emails to finally get in contact with the person you wanted to connect with.

Now, you can do that same networking with a few clicks on LinkedIn.

Having that kind of technology at your fingertips is powerful. Use it to get a leg up in an interview or new client pitch. Prior to going in, look for little kernels of information on her profile. Maybe she used to work in the town you currently live in, or graduated from the same university. Finding things that can establish even a small connection can make a big impact in your interactions.

Focus on building a foundation of professional contacts. Identify key people in your industry, and ask if they'd be willing to meet you for coffee. Remember, the answer is always no if you don't ask.

Use every opportunity to connect with people. You never know who you might be sitting next to on an airplane or train. Don't just sit down and immediately put your headphones on. It's possible that the person next to you could be an invaluable contact.

Usspire founder Mina Salib tells a story about attending a fashion show during which he was seated next to an average-looking guy wearing a T-shirt and jeans. Because he looked like a nobody, Salib didn't bother initiating a conversation.

You can imagine his surprise when that "nobody" got up on stage and introduced himself as Steve Madden, the famous shoe designer.

Reach out to anyone you want to talk to. Send a personalized email to each person, not an impersonal email blast to your entire wish list. Again, do your research and find a commonality that will bring a little more creativity to the conversation when you're making the ask.

When you take the time to put a little bit of effort in, chances are good it will be much more well-received. Just don't get all stressed about reaching out in the first place. The worst thing they can do is say no.

You also want to take advantage of less formal networking opportunities that are part of your day-to-day living.

Our friend Gretchen was a professional couch surfer for almost five years after college. Although she got her engineering degree, she didn't have a clue about what she wanted to do with her life. For months, she floated from job to job, crashing in somebody's guest room or on their couch for a month here and a month there.

One day, Kate's sister dragged Gretchen to a party where she met a girl whose dad is a major executive for an engineering firm out in Colorado. Because they hit it off so well, the girl called her dad from the party and basically told him that he needed to hire Gretchen immediately. Long story short, Gretchen sent in her resume, nailed the interview, and now has the coolest job of anyone we know, traveling all around the country and working on amazing projects.

Spend less time sitting around watching Netflix on a Saturday night. Get your ass off the couch and go to the event you've been invited to. You never know what connections you could be making while there.

RESUME BASICS

According to *Business Insider*, it takes recruiters a mere six seconds to determine whether you're a yay or a nay for a particular job.

Even if you're getting an interview through somebody you know, you're still expected to have a resume that succinctly sells your unique skill sets. Also, be aware that the majority of resumes go through electric screening that is just pulling for keywords. It's typically not even reviewed by a human at first. That's why it's so critical to make sure the words on the page have meaning.

To ensure your resume is as flawless as possible, do the following:

- ⏻ Include your name and contact information in bold at the top.
- ⏻ Stick to traditional fonts such as Arial, 11 or 12 point.
- ⏻ Create your unique value proposition, but be explicit about how it

will benefit them. Don't say, "I'm the best at SEO (search engine optimization)," but rather, "Here's how I do SEO, but I'll prove it at your company by doing X, Y, or Z."

- ⏻ Begin each sentence with an action verb, such as *designed*, *implemented*, *coordinated*, *applied*, and so on.
- ⏻ Lay off the excessive punctuation and emojis. We can't believe we have to say this, but it happens.
- ⏻ If there are specific attributes that the company is looking for in their job description, change the wording around in your resume to tailor fit that job. This means that it's more difficult to mass submit your resume, but if you're looking for quality over quantity, then that's the way to go.
- ⏻ Keep it to one page. If you're higher than a director level, you can opt for two.
- ⏻ Tailor your resume to a format that's industry appropriate.
- ⏻ Check for spelling and grammatical errors by reading it out loud, and always have someone else proofread it.
- ⏻ Try a mental exercise where you "pay yourself" one hundred dollars for every word you delete without sacrificing the point. This is a favorite tip from *Dilbert* creator Scott Adams.

Some companies will say to include a video, photo, or infographic. Following instructions is critical, but if they didn't ask for something outside the norm, it's best to stick with the traditional resume as your starting point.

In an era where we obsess over putting our personal stamp

on everything, we understand how boring the traditional resume format might seem.

There are some situations that are the exception to the rule. But even if you are applying for a graphic design position and want your resume to reflect your mad Illustrator and Photoshop skills, be sure to also include a plain-text version for the interviewer.

In doing so, you demonstrate your amazing creative prowess but also an awareness and respect for commonly accepted methodologies and practices.

The following pages illustrate a "before and after" example from our friend, whom we'll call Aaron Samuels. Kate got his original resume in her hands and tweaked it to make a stronger impact.

WHAT TO COVER IN YOUR COVER LETTER

Put thought into what you are saying. Avoid boring templates. State clearly and precisely how you can bring value to the company or project, but don't remove all traces of your personality.

Rob has gotten a job not because of his resume that was attached to the email but because of the content of the email itself.

Aaron B. Samuels

3001 Main Street
Baltimore, MD 21218

(C) 555-555-5555
AaronBSamuels@gmail.com

Summary
MBA and candidate for Masters in Management of Sport Industries with a diverse background in creating value and solutions via SAP, Excel, and cross-functional planning and collaboration. Proven leader with a wealth of experience managing individuals, teams, and processes throughout the supply chain. Customer oriented, team player with experience reporting and tracking multiple programs simultaneously from procurement to test stand delivery including international logistics and communications.

Education

01/2015-Present **University of New Haven,** West Haven, CT
Candidate for Master of Science in Management of Sport Industries

08/2009- 12/2010 **University of Tennessee, Haslam School of Business,** Knoxville, TN
Masters of Business Administration; Marketing, Entrepreneurship & Innovation

08/2005 -12/2008 **Rollins College,** Winter Park, FL
Bachelor of Arts; Psychology

Work Experience

12/2011-Present **Pratt & Whitney, United Technologies Corporation,** East Hartford, CT
Global leader in the design, manufacture, and support of turbine engines.
Senior Materials Analyst, Turbine Module Center, East Hartford, CT
- Utilize SAP and Solumina to troubleshoot and solve a multitude of issues across warehousing, inspection, procurement, receiving and production planning in order to improve lead times and delivery reliability
- Lead learning opportunities and source individuals to cross-functional, issue resolution teams from areas such as procurement, warehousing, inspection, engineering, and suppliers
- Continuously reducing lead time of production order creation and material sourcing as well as material shortages via process improvement methodologies and improved order qualification standards
- Improve employee morale, communication, and engagement through inclusive activities that break down silos within Project Material Control

Materials Analyst, Turbine Module Center, East Hartford, CT
- Led the Employee Spot Survey Action Team: Communication and Teamwork and determined the root cause issues and presented clear solutions at the managerial, supervisorial, and employee levels
- Led the 2014 Roles and Responsibilities team and established clear roles for incoming employees and laid the ground work for improved growth and development opportunities, increased MFA scores, and decreased turnover within Project Material Control
- Developed reduced lead time initiatives as a member of a cross functional value stream mapping event
- Integrated into the turbine module center to support all commercial and military programs as the airfoil focal point for Project Material Control

Materials Analyst, Compression Systems Module Center, Middletown, CT
- Received MFA scores of 6 and 7 out of a possible 7 from programs I supported
- Developed employee centric solutions to improve market feedback analysis of a young organization as a member of the Skills Development process improvement team
- Conceived and worked recovery plans to the PMC focal point to the fan blade module of the PurePower Airbus 320 developmental program to ensure delivery for critical engine certification with our Japanese partners JAEC
- Managed procurement to test material responsibilities of the high and low pressure compressors for the FT4000 Next-generation Aero-derivative Gas Turbine developmental testing program

01/2011-11/2011 **Ocwen Financial Corporation,** West Palm Beach, FL
Provider of mortgage loan servicing, special servicing, and asset management services.
Contract Management Coordinator
- Prepared various documents pertaining to mortgage loans, modifications, and chain of title including but not limited to: foreclosure and bankruptcy affidavits, modification agreements, assignments and satisfaction of mortgage, and power of attorneys
- Reviewed, verified, and executed legal documents prepared by internal and external parties as required
- Prepared daily, weekly, and monthly reporting with MS Excel and proprietary software
- Identified, researched, and resolved document discrepancies for 100+ legal affidavits daily

BEFORE (PAGE 1)

06/2010-08/2010 **Hibiscus Children's Center**, Jensen Beach, FL
Shelter for children who are abused, abandoned, and neglected.
Marketing and Public Relations Intern
- Developed a yearlong marketing plan for Hibiscus' 25 year anniversary celebration
- Researched, composed, and distributed a number of articles to the local media for the purpose of informing the public about the services Hibiscus offers
- Featured as a guest columnist in Scripps' Stuart News newspaper for a piece about the significance of Hibiscus' 25 years in the community
- Created social media campaigns to inform and raise awareness about Hibiscus' mission and services
- Helped develop a historical timeline of Hibiscus for a promotional book to thank donors and highlight Hibiscus' impact in the community

Other Experience
06/2002-08/2010 **Martin County School Board**, Stuart, FL
Supervisor/Lifeguard
09/2009-03/2010 **Rita's Italian Ice**, Knoxville, TN
Marketing Intern
09/2009-11/2009 **Tennessee Traditions**, Knoxville, TN
Game Day Sales Associate
03/2009-0 8/2009 **Carpentry Plus**, Palm City, FL
Assistant
08/2008-08/2009 **Martin County Aquatics/Martin County High School**, Stuart, FL
Assistant Swim Coach
01/2007-08/2007 **J. Crew**, Orlando, FL
Support Staff

Professional Education
09/2015	**Leading Teams: Dealing with Conflict**
05/2015	**Leadership Development II: Understanding and Managing Change**
10/2014	**Influencing and Motivating Others, Harvard**
09/2014	**Getting Results without Authority**
10/2013	**Avoiding Bribery and Corruption: A Global Overview**
04/2013	**Valuing and Responding to Employees Concerns**
03/2013	**Careful Communication**
12/2012	**Lean Advancement the 'Toyota Way'**
11/2012	**Supply Chain Management Fundamentals**
11/2012	**Process Management – Process Certification and Process Robustness**
11/2012	**Managing Change, Harvard**
03/2012	**Intellectual Property Training for Engineers**
12/2011	**Value Stream Mapping**

Skills Acquired
Computer
- Extensive work with SAP and Solumina
- Proficient with Microsoft Office Suite: PowerPoint, Word, and Excel
- Some experience with SPSS, StatPlus, and Decision Tree
- Very familiar with social media outlets Facebook, Twitter, LinkedIn, etc.

Presentation/ Organizational
- Able to plan, prioritize, and mange time effectively
- Communicate clearly and concisely through spoken and written communication
- Able to work effectively under pressure

Personal
- Able to overcome mental barriers and push myself further than most
- Easily adaptable to a variety of circumstances
- Effective listener, personable, and able to work effectively in a team

BEFORE (PAGE 2)

Aaron Samuels, MBA

✉ AaronBSamuels@gmail.com | ☏ 555-555-5555 | 🖥 https://www.linkedin.com/in/AaronBSamuels

Senior supply chain professional with over four years of experience at a top Fortune 500 company leading cross-functional teams through ever-changing demands. Exceptional project and task manager who is able to manage priorities and team members through clear communication and strategic problem solving.

Proficiencies:

SAP ECC ✦ Solumina ✦ Teamcenter ✦ Microsoft Office Suite: PowerPoint, Word, Excel, Access ✦ SAP BI
✦Presenting ✦ Time management ✦ Project management ✦ Team leadership ✦ Analytical thinking

Senior Materials Analyst, Turbine Module Center   (2015→Present)
Pratt & Whitney, East Hartford, CT

- Provided support for an estimated $24.6m worth of turbine airfoil inventory and support services across 10+ developmental programs and over 100 different engine tests throughout 2015
- Utilize SAP and Solumina to troubleshoot and solve issues across warehousing, quality inspection, procurement, receiving, and production planning in order to improve lead times and delivery reliability
- Lead learning opportunities and source individuals to cross-functional, issue-resolution teams from areas such as procurement, warehousing, quality inspection, engineering, and suppliers
- Continuously reducing lead time of production order creation, material sourcing, and material shortages as an ACE Associate (Six Sigma Green Belt equivalent) via process improvement and streamlining order-qualification standards

Materials Analyst, Turbine Module Center   (2013→2015)
Pratt & Whitney, East Hartford, CT

- Increased management favorability scores by 33% as leader of the 2014 Employee Spot Survey Action Team: Communication and Teamwork which determined root cause issues and presented clear solutions at the managerial, supervisorial, and employee levels
- Decreased Project Material Control turnover by 50% in 2015 after leading the 2014 Roles and Responsibilities team that established clear roles for incoming employees and laid the ground work for improved growth and development opportunities, suggested employee training methods and increased MFA scores
- Supported the delivery of approximately $18.3m worth of hardware and support services per year as the commercial and military programs airfoil focal point

Materials Planner, Compression Systems Module Center   (2011→2013)
Pratt & Whitney, Middletown, CT

- Exceeded yearly KPI expectations to earn MFA scores of 6 and 7 out of a possible 7 through exceptional customer service and project management to meet program deadlines
- Ensured the delivery of approximately $2.6m worth of critical of hardware and support by creating and working recovery plans with our Japanese partners JAEC as the Project Material Control focal point to the fan blade module of the PurePower Airbus A320 developmental program
- Managed $5.3m worth of procurement to test material and support services of the high and low pressure compressors for the FT4000 Next-generation Aero-derivative Gas Turbine developmental testing program

Contract Management Coordinator   (Jan 2011→Nov 2011)
Ocwen Financial Corporation, West Palm Beach, FL

- Developed daily, weekly, and monthly reporting with MS Excel and proprietary software on special assignment due to identified technical proficiency and project management skills
- Identified, researched, and resolved document discrepancies for 100+ legal affidavits daily compared to the average of 50 for contract coordinators by developing a personal system of organization

Master of Science; Management of Sport Industries   (Dec 2015)
University of New Haven, West Haven, CT
Master of Business Administration; Marketing, Entrepreneurship & Innovation   (Dec 2010)
University of Tennessee, Haslam College of Business, Knoxville, TN
Bachelor of Arts; Psychology   (Dec 2008)
Rollins College, Winter Park, FL

AFTER

He knew enough about the person on the receiving end after doing a bit of online research to include some humor in his note. Thus, Rob could humanize his strong, traditional resume.

Often, the creativity comes in the delivery.

NAILING THE INTERVIEW

We're going straight to the top on this one. Here's what *Forbes* had to say:

1. Wear something appropriate. Yes, we sound like a broken record, but if you want to be taken seriously as a professional, then dress like one.

2. Arrive with plenty of time to spare, but don't walk in the door until about five minutes before your scheduled interview time. It conveys the impression that you are professional and organized.

3. Bring extra copies of your resume.

4. Do your due diligence. Before you even step foot in the door, use your Internet skills to research the company, position, and industry. This is where LinkedIn can be your best friend. Identify someone who is already working there, and ask if he or she would meet you for coffee so you can get a handle on the culture and environment.

5. Be aware of your body language. Planting your feet and holding your head level makes you appear confidently in control.

6. Ask smart questions. The research you did beforehand will come in handy at this point in your conversation.

7. Smile. Honestly, lighten up! You don't want to come off as unconfident, petrified, or indifferent.

8. Sweep your social media. As we stated before, delete anything that your grandma would not approve of. It's a standard procedure nowadays for hiring managers to creep on your feeds.

9. Sell yourself confidently, but don't be cocky about it.

10. Follow up with a thank-you note that summarizes your qualifications and emphasizes your interest. Emails are acceptable. Handwritten notes are better.

We're also adding a few "duh" points of our own:

1. Never answer a call, text, or email during an interview. Set your phone to DND (do not disturb) before you even step through the door.

2. Do not bring anyone with you to a job interview. If you need a ride, the driver will have to wait in the car or go to a nearby coffee shop until you are done. No one should ever see him or her. It might also

be wise to pretend he or she is an Uber driver so you appear more self-sufficient.

3. Don't badmouth anyone. This includes past and current employers. "It wasn't the best fit" is always a good default answer when asked why you're leaving your current job.

4. Your needs in an interview are not important. What *is* important is conveying that you can fill the gap *they* need filled.

General life rule: The person giving the money is the one whose needs matter. You get paid to meet needs.

During your interview, a common question you'll be asked is: "What are your weaknesses?" Pick something that's not going to be the downfall of you but is a legitimate weakness.

Don't reply with a lame answer, like, "Oh, my biggest weakness is I work too hard," or, "I can't turn off my computer and stop working when I get home."

Kate would say her weakness is impatience and a lack of soft skills. However, she'd elaborate by explaining how she works on both on a regular basis—in both her personal and professional life—to demonstrate how she's addressing her weaknesses head-on.

Recently, a friend of ours was in the process of negotiating a job offer.

"I think I want to ask for more money," she confided to us, seeking advice.

We asked her to forward the email thread that had been going back and forth between her and the hiring manager.

As we read through, it became clear she had already given notice at her previous job and had accepted this new one along with the salary they offered. Thus, she had eliminated any sort of presumed leverage she had, and the hiring manager knew it.

Use this as a cautionary tale not to tip your hand too early on, especially when it comes to negotiating a salary.

If anybody asks what you make at your current job, deflect.

If they press and ask for a specific number, deflect again.

"This is the range that I'm currently interviewing in. Is this within the range of your budget?" is how you want to respond. Diffuse the situation by putting it back on them.

It's also fair to factor in your vacation time and any other benefits that are part of your compensation package at your current job.

If you're still stumped as to what to ask for, use Glassdoor to get insights on the average salary range being offered for that position. Another great resource is "The Ultimate Guide for Getting a Raise and Boosting Your Salary" from IWillTeachYouToBeRich.com.

When you are finally at the point to negotiate, divide up what you want to ask for, and ask for one piece at a time. Get the answer on one part before moving on. Studies show you are much more likely to get what you want when you ask for it this way.

WHAT THE CORPORATE WORLD EXPECTS OF YOU

Whether you are just entering the workforce or approaching age forty, there is an expectation that you'll just get how the corporate business world works.

But as Felice, a senior vice president at a major financial firm with forty-five years of experience, put it, "So often when people enter the workplace, the managers forget that people aren't born knowing stuff."

While it could be applied across the board to all generations, Millennials experience an amplified gap in this area. Perhaps because we've been focused on keeping up with rapidly changing technology, or maybe due to the deemphasizing of in-person interaction in all parts of our day, we struggle to segue our understanding of how the modern world works with the understanding of how a company that's been embracing the same approaches since 1975 works.

Some of these expectations can be easily conveyed on paper, others are subtler and best explored through face-to-face interaction with a mentor or advocate. Many vary by company.

Expect a learning curve. Start with a working knowledge of the basics, such as the handshake. If you aren't 100 percent sure you have a solid handshake, Google it and practice.

It might seem simple and even a bit stupid to be talking about this, but there are a lot of handshake fouls we experience regularly, by people of all generations. There is a not a single, highly respected and successful leader who has not mastered the art of the handshake. Don't undervalue its importance.

Other examples of basic, proper business etiquette are described below.

DRESS FOR SUCCESS

Blah, blah, blah, I get it, you're probably thinking. We hear you. Sadly, though, most of our generation does not. Lest you're still unsure, research shows that what you wear even affects your performance, according to a study published in the *New York Times.* Basically, it found that young women seem to lose intellectual focus when they're self-conscious about what they're wearing. So, leave the yoga pants and "I am my own happy hour" T-shirt at home. Dress for the job you want, or better yet, above the job you want. At a bare minimum, keep a blazer in your cubicle or office. You never know when you might get called into a meeting with the CEO.

DON'T SWEAT THE SMALL STUFF

If the food in the cafeteria is shitty, keep your mouth shut and brown-bag it instead. A good rule of thumb is no complaining unless you've developed an accompanying solution, or a request for help finding a solution. Choose these battles wisely. There's an old saying about how it's not worth winning the battle if it will make you lose the war. If you have the energy to focus on how bad the food is, that will likely prompt questions about whether you're focused enough on what really matters: your job.

BE NICE TO THE SECRETARY

It's a general rule of thumb that if you get along with

the secretary/admin, life in the office will go a whole lot smoother. Treat everyone with the same respect from day one. It doesn't matter what his or her job title is. This is equally as important during the interview process. If you left a bad impression on the admin, your follow-up call/ note/email will most likely not be getting through to the person hiring you.

WHILE YOU'RE AT IT, BE NICE TO THE JANITOR, TOO

Everyone deserves to be treated with dignity and respect. Period. Not to mention, the janitor is the person who is going to save your ass when you've accidentally lost your key to your office on the morning of a major presentation. According to *Forbes*, how your CEO treats the janitor is a pretty good illustration of the DNA of the company. Take note.

BE RESPECTFUL OF PEOPLE'S SPACE

Whether it's a cubicle or office, don't just barge your way into someone's space. Approach quietly and knock before entering.

SIMMER DOWN BEFORE HITTING "SEND"

Do not send angry emails. When it's necessary to express your displeasure over something, write out a response in a blank email and let it marinate for a while. Overnight is ideal, but if time is limited, at least go outside for a five-minute walk to get some fresh air and calm down.

UNDERSTAND HOW YOUR MILLENNIAL "MULTITASKING" MIGHT BE INTERPRETED

You might think you're showing off some serious multitasking skills by trying to Google an answer during a meeting, but more than likely, the room is going to assume you're texting or on Snapchat and therefore not paying attention.

A safer approach would be to ask the presenter, "Would you like me to quickly Google an answer on my phone?" That way, you still show initiative, but you eliminate all misconceptions about what you are doing underneath the table.

Another good habit to get into is bringing a pen and paper pad to the meeting rather than relying on your phone to take notes.

That's so old fashioned, you say?

Well, maybe, but not doing so is always misconceived as not paying attention, particularly with an older crowd or senior execs. Writing on your phone, or even laptop, may give the wrong impression. Plus, research has shown that you're much more likely to remember key points of a presentation, dates, or statistics from a meeting if you write notes by hand verses typing them. Princeton University's Pam Mueller and UCLA's Daniel Oppenheimer conducted experiments on students that showed writing by hand encouraged people to process and summarize what is being said, rather than just regurgitating it.

True, Millennials ~~are innately good at multitasking and~~ find it easier to jump quickly from task to task than older generations; but it just comes off poorly in a conference room.

So why the strikethrough in the above sentence? Because multitasking is a myth.

We both love to argue that we are totally capable of multitasking. But the reality is we are just exceptionally good at task-switching. (By the way, be prepared for that to go away as you get older. For most of us, it will.)

Dr. Jeremy Hunter, an expert in workplace productivity and professor at the Drucker School of Management, has found that multitasking damages your productivity, your relationships, and even **your brain.** Feel free to Google more about the science of it, but in non-science-y terms, it messes with your ability to learn, make decisions, and remember things.

Maybe this is why we can never decide where to go for dinner?

MANAGE YOUR RESOURCES: HEALTH, MONEY, AND TIME

We were going to call this section "How to Be Better at Your Job," but really, that's only the half of it.

You can't just fly through life without a plan. Organization is going to be the key to keeping your sanity and staying on top of things. You must be organized and prepared, and have control of your life outside of your job, to be able to dedicate appropriate energy *to* your job.

Learn the art of balancing. Understand how this concept goes both ways. It's never good when your job drains so much life out of you that the only thing you're good for at the end of the day is plopping down on the couch and watching mindless television.

Commit to a lifestyle that embraces healthy personal **and** professional choices.

GET YOUR PRIORITIES IN ORDER

Every Monday we start off by planning not only the day but also the week. Rob prefers to type everything up in a Word document that he prints out, adding notes as necessary.

By the time Friday rolls around, he feels a sense of accomplishment by looking at everything he's checked off. Anything outstanding is put on the following week's agenda.

Alternatively, Kate and her friend Regina are calendar-obsessed. If it's not on the calendar, it's not happening.

Figure out what works best for you. Maybe it's using a traditional day planner, your Google calendar, or an app on your phone. Find a way to stay organized to keep yourself accountable. It eliminates the chances of missing a deadline, meeting, or conference call, as well as unnecessary anxiety and stress.

YOU SNOOZE, YOU LOSE

Wake up early. Don't wait until the last second and smack the hell out of your snooze button every morning.

All that does is create a frantic rush: rush to the shower, rush out the door, rush to work.

Give yourself ample time to get ready. It eliminates the stress that results from having to rush and replaces it with a healthy energy level for whatever lies ahead.

Getting into the habit of waking up earlier also will

most likely dissuade you from closing the bar during the weekday.

Another pro-tip: waking up at a similar time on the weekends, within an hour or two of your weekday rising time, will help reinforce the habit.

YOU ARE WHAT YOU EAT

"Work that only comes from the head isn't any good. Watch a great musician play a show. Watch a great leader give a speech. You'll see what I mean."

It's a line from Austin Kleon's book *Steal Like an Artist* that speaks to taking care of your body as well, making sure it's being trained and shaped and worked just like your brain would be at the workplace.

When it comes to healthy eating habits, find what works best for you.

Due to stomach issues, Kate trained herself to eat foods that were healthier out of sheer necessity. For example, she used to hate sweet potatoes. Her only exposure to them was that awful Thanksgiving marshmallow casserole her family insisted on serving every year. Repulsive.

But she knew that the sweet potato itself was a very healthy food option. So, she started off disguising them with other things, usually mixed with other mashed potatoes or standard French fries, until she eventually tricked herself into liking them on their own. Now, they're a staple in her diet.

MOVE IT OR LOSE IT

Yadda, yadda, yadda. Look, we all know how important exercise is for a healthy mind, body, and soul, so stop making excuses—get off the couch and do something.

Rob trains for marathons and rowing regattas. Kate prefers quick-hit videos in the morning, so she doesn't feel guilty all day about trying to fit a workout in. Both of us love having an "accountabilibuddy" to take some of the choice out of whether we're getting to the gym.

It doesn't matter what it is: cycling, lifting, yoga, whatever.

Regular physical activity sets you up with a healthy body. You're sharper, generally happier, and more energetic. If you want to put your best foot forward in your professional and personal life, you've got to take good care of yourself. Otherwise, you're wasting one of the best resources you have: *you.*

POWERING DOWN

That's just a fancy way of saying *vacation* or *PTO* (paid

time off), but everybody has a different idea of what it means to power down from your job and how often you should be doing it.

For Rob, after seventy-two hours he's ready to get back to work, rejuvenated and feeling creative. He kind of sucks at taking long vacations because it's hard for him to fully disconnect for extended periods of time.

On the other hand, Kate could be completely focused for three straight weeks without a break, then put her phone away while on vacation and not look at it at all.

It depends on the circumstances, but sometimes you must force yourself to disconnect to recharge your batteries. But take notice of how you feel after you've experienced time off. Do you feel relaxed or stressed by the time it's over?

For some people, finding your happy place might take five days. For others, it may take two weeks. Just listen to your body. There's no point in taking a full two weeks of vacation if you need Xanax to ward off the anxiety attacks. In that case, you'd be better served taking a day off here and there, or maybe a long weekend.

Whether you're prone to leisurely PTO or can't stand the very thought of it, one thing to consider is whether your industry is prone to being busier during certain times of the year. If that's the case, it's probably wise to consider waiting until a calmer period to take time off.

GIVE THANKS

Get into the habit of sending thank-you notes. This applies to your personal life, too, not just your professional one. The best way to make an impact on your friend's parents who were kind enough to let you get drunk on their boat/ stay at their house/drink their wine is to send a handwritten thank-you card. Start with the word *you*, as in "You were so kind to...," be specific about how you benefitted from that kindness, and then thank them for it.

EXERCISING YOUR FISCAL RESPONSIBILITY

If you're stressed out about something at home, it's going to creep its way into your work.

This includes your finances. It's hard to stay focused on a major pitch when all you can think about is how to dodge another call from the collection agency.

Not spending money like a drunken sailor is an effective way to eliminate the unnecessary stress that can result from being financially irresponsible.

Make it a point to develop good saving habits early on.

Always have three to six months' worth of cash on hand in the event of an emergency, like when the ax falls on your job or the motor in your Honda blows up.

Start saving for your 401(k)-plan beginning with your very first paycheck. What you can save at age twenty-five will have the magic of compounded interest by the time you are thirty-five.

There are plenty of resources you can find today that will teach you how to manage your dollars and cents. Talk to your parents, responsible friends, or even a financial advisor to get helpful tips on what will work best for you.

When it comes to fiscal responsibility, beware: Sometimes people will insist that you pay heed to common clichés about finances that aren't always true, such as the following.

CREDIT CARDS ARE BAD
How is that a misconception?

Credit cards can help you build your credit score so you can do bigger and better.

Meaning what?

A good credit score means lower interest rates, higher limits on lending, better insurance rates, and cool perks. When used responsibly, credit cards can become an asset to you.

Define "responsibly."

Treat them like debit cards. Pay them off every month, or every week if that works better for you. If you don't, you'll end up paying up to three times more for that twenty-dollar sweater you scored on sale, thanks to the added interest. Also, find a program that gives you cash back, and you could earn 1.5 percent on everything you purchase throughout the year. For us, that means we get a head start on our Christmas presents.

RENTING IS JUST THROWING AWAY MONEY
How is that a misconception?

There are many instances in which renting makes better financial sense than buying.

Like when?

If you tend to job-hop every two or three years, or don't want to commit yourself to a certain city for an extended period, renting may be a good idea. Maybe you live in a city where you can't afford to own property, but your job is an important calculated step in your career. Perhaps the onsite gym/trainer/shuttle/coffee/dry cleaner are conveniences that enable you to stay focused on advancing yourself. (Note: this does not say "stay focused on impressing your friends.")

Yeah, but everyone says it's stupid to rent.

What's stupid is how much money you could potentially lose if you buy a house and move before it has ample time to appreciate. Calculate how much money you would need to put down (20 percent is the average), plus closing costs, interest you're paying on the loan, property taxes, and unexpected maintenance costs, and then compare that to what you would be paying in rent every year.

What do you mean by maintenance costs?

When then roof starts to leak or the hot water tank goes are just two examples. That's cash out of your pocket to fix these.

There are instances where buying a house could serve as a great investment and opportunity. Just do some homework to make sure it's the best choice for you, given your current and future career goals. Consider the trajectory

of property values where you're looking and other investment options, too.

ONLY RICH PEOPLE HAVE A MAID

How is that a misconception?

There could be a serious time/convenience trade-off that
comes from hiring a cleaning lady.

How can I figure that out?

First determine if you're spending three, four, or more
hours a week cleaning the house when you could be doing
something more productive with your time.

Define "productive."

Think about whether the time you're spending cleaning
the house is taking away from valuable downtime on
the weekend, energy you could be investing in an extra
project at work, or time you have just to think. We tend
to feel as if time spent thinking doesn't count as being
productive, since there's usually no output to show for it,
but focused thinking is a critical part to understanding
and evolving the big picture. If you're the type of person
who can't stand looking at dirt, but are legitimately too
busy to clean, then hiring someone affordable to do it for

you can be a worthwhile option.

Knowing what you're worth per hour is an important number to figure out. Then ask yourself, *Is my time worth this task, or does it make better sense to outsource it?*

MASTER THE ART OF CONVERSATION AND PUBLIC SPEAKING

This is such an important skill to master early on that it's slightly disturbing that more universities don't make it a core requirement for any degree.

Anyone can learn how to be an engaging speaker when given the proper tools. But even the best public speakers received training at some point in their life. Having these skills is critical for being better at life in general.

It's part of finding your voice, the foundation of getting your idea heard and selling it. Getting better at verbally representing yourself is one of the best investments you'll ever make.

Most major cities have a program called Toastmasters. It's a nonprofit organization comprised of people from all walks of life and experiences who support each other in the pursuit of better public speaking and leadership skills through repetitive practice. You can check out their website at Toastmasters.org to find a nearby chapter.

If you're feeling shy when in unfamiliar surroundings, head somewhere where you stand in line with others—the bathroom, buffet, bar—and start a conversation. You already have something in common. You are at the same event, waiting for the same thing.

Still at a loss for words?

In his book *How to Fail at Almost Everything*, cartoonist and *Dilbert* creator Scott Adams offers seven basic rules to master any conversation:

1. **Ask questions.**

2. **Don't complain (much).**

3. **Don't talk about boring experiences such as TV, meals, dreams, et cetera.**

4. **Don't dominate the conversation; let others talk.**

5. **Don't get stuck on a topic; keep moving.**

6. **Planning is useful, but it isn't a conversation.**

7. **Keep the sad stories short, especially medical stories.**

We'll add a few more, paraphrased from *Adulting: How to Become a Grown-Up in 468 Easy(ish) Steps* by Kelly Williams Brown:

1. Avoid topics you feel intensely about to avoid the conversation feeling like a lecture.

2. Leave them wanting more, not less, of you.

3. Don't comment on other people's bodies, such as their sunburn, the cast on their foot, or that they are tall, pregnant, or look tired, unless they say something first. They are probably already self-conscious and sick of talking about it.

4. Don't talk about your own body. It makes other people uncomfortable.

5. If someone says something offensive or cruel that cannot be ignored, say, "I'm sure you didn't mean that the way it came out," and then change the topic immediately.

We talked earlier about using *The Skimm* as a valuable tool that can help keep you up to date on what's going on in the world. Current events are a great topic for interesting conversation. It doesn't matter if you couldn't care less about what's trending—the point is that it helps you to relate to other people and, in turn, appear more relatable.

But while it's important to be interesting, don't be so interesting that you become a punchline.

KEEP A TAME SOCIAL MEDIA PRESENCE

Keep your digital signature "Grandma approved." If that's not enough to convince you, take a minute to think about your dream job.

Now, imagine yourself as the CEO, and look at your social media feed.

Does it come off right? How would it be perceived by your employees, stockholders, and clients? How would you like that picture of you slinging back shots of Jägermeister on the home page of the *Huffington Post* or the *Wall Street Journal*?

Don't make the mistake of assuming you're safe because you privatized your account when you first opened it. Privacy settings are constantly being changed by the provider, leaving you open to indecent exposure.

More than enough people have been disqualified for a job because of inappropriate or offensive social media posts. Our friend Karen was involved with a round of interviews being conducted by her company. They put a really strong candidate on the short list until they came across his profile photo: double barrel middle fingers while scuba diving.

In case you were wondering, he didn't get the job.

HAVING A HANDLE ON TECHNOLOGY

Technological prowess extends beyond a social media feed.

Make sure you understand your way around the basics of Microsoft Office and a computer operating system.

On the flip side, do an internal audit to verify that you're not already starting down the path of being technology adverse. There's a small subset of Digital Natives that have completely rejected it, eschewing not only social media but widely accepted digital platforms as well.

If Snapchat isn't your thing, that's okay. But at least get what Scott Adams calls a "hobby level understanding of technology" so you aren't completely out of touch.

HOW TO BE A PROFESSIONAL PROFESSIONAL
BE PROACTIVE

Taking a cue from *Lean In* author Cheryl Sandberg, don't be afraid to ask for what you need and what you deserve. A good way to do this is to equip yourself with preparation strategies we talked about earlier in the chapter.

Script it, pitch it, then tailor the message depending on your audience.

Practice asking for things that you want. Go out and test your skills in real-life, low-risk scenarios. For example, negotiate the price on a car, try to get a better and bigger credit limit or updated perks on your credit card, or go to a garage sale and haggle on the price of something you want. The point is to be proactive in your practicing until you become more comfortable at doing it. That way, when it counts, you'll have the confidence, poise, and knowledge necessary to present and win your case.

INVEST IN YOURSELF

Shark Tank panelist and real-estate empress Barbara Cochran was once asked what someone should invest in if they had $10,000 lying around.

"That's a ridiculous question," she said. "The only thing worth investing in is yourself. And so the real question is... what do you feel passionate about? Is there an angle you could work that would make you some money?"

If you aren't willing to invest in yourself, why should anyone else invest in you?

Enough said.

Obviously, emotional intelligence encompasses a lot of what is going to enable you to be levelheaded and productive in the workplace. It's the glue that will keep your team together. It's been proven that emotionally intelligent people are more likely to have more motivated and productive staffs.

A significant way to improve your emotional intelligence is by having mentors and people who are sometimes older but always wiser than you that can be trusted for candid feedback. This is someone who will call you out when you're being overly dramatic, or talk you down when you're completely freaking out.

Chelsea Handler once posted a video to Facebook where she admitted she had gotten really jealous of another woman who had been hired for a job she wanted. Instead of obsessing or spending countless hours on the phone in consultation with her tribe, she picked one trusted person to vent to and then got over it.

As she put it: "I never blow out someone else's candle to make mine brighter."

If you're telling ten friends the same story over and over and over again, you're wasting valuable time. It takes away from productivity you could be having in your job or other areas of your life.

Former Olympian and NFL player Jeremy Bloom offers another rule that can sharpen your emotional intelligence: when you're upset about something, set an appropriate deadline at which point you must get over it. For him, that's usually forty-eight hours.

Both are examples of how you can develop a heightened emotional intelligence, which in turn flexes the mental muscles necessary to keep you focused on the right path.

Also, you'll find great value in taking a Teflon approach—let a lot of criticism and negativity just slide right off you. Not everything has to be addressed, and not everyone has to like you. If you don't like someone and he or she doesn't like you, that is an agreement, not a problem.

AVOID BEING "JUST ANOTHER DAMN MILLENNIAL"

Most of what's been written by Millennials for Millennials is, in a word, defensive. "Yeah, we are these things you say, and we don't think it's a bad thing," is a common theme.

Stop wasting your breath trying to defend yourself. Focus your efforts on using your unique skill set to *prove* your value and worth. Again, communication is key. Take action and seek out advice. When you commit to being better at life, you're going to learn a lot. In turn, that learning will open countless doors that lead to a more positive, healthy, and impactful future.

CHAPTER 1 ACTION ITEMS

- ⏻ Perfect your personal elevator pitch.
- ⏻ Negotiate something of low importance to practice negotiation.
- ⏻ Buy a notebook and pen that you like to use in meetings.

CHAPTER 2

· ·

UNDERSTANDING BASIC LEADERSHIP STYLES

· ·

THE RELATIONSHIP YOU'RE going to have with coworkers and management is going to succeed or fail depending largely on one thing: communication.

Reading sensationalized headlines that lament "Why Can't Millennials Grow Up?" and how to deal with "A Generation of Idle Trophy Kids" would lead anyone to believe that we just don't give a damn about anything.

In general, that's anything but the truth.

A recent Gallup poll found that 44 percent of Millennials who report that their manager holds regular meetings with them feel engaged at work. On the flip side, only 20 percent of Millennials who did not meet regularly with their manager felt engaged.

Clearly, there's a communication problem here. Neither side seems to understand what the other needs to work most productively. What a more seasoned worker would see as being needy is what our generation finds necessary to be a productive employee.

To bridge the gap, you need savvy communication skills tailored to a variety of personality types.

Express to your manager that you want constructive criticism on a consistent basis so she doesn't think you're just fishing for praise. Frame your request around his or her needs—not yours—by saying, "I'd love to meet with you each week for fifteen minutes to discuss my performance so that I can make sure I'm meeting your expectations."

The important thing to remember, though, is that the goal isn't to change the other person. Your goal is to be smart enough to quickly identify who you're dealing with in order to create a win-win.

However, we realize that there are going to be some people and managers you encounter that just straight up suck.

Consider the following your navigation guide.

PROFILE YOUR BOSSES

As you embark on your illustrious career, it is most likely that your boss will be heavily identified with one of these three personality types, but expect some crossover. Rarely is someone so one-dimensional.

Remember, though: It's not enough to identify what category your boss falls into. Your success depends on being able to understand his or her values and principles as well. Once you figure that out you'll be better equipped for anticipating what to expect, how to adapt to his or her style, and when to *just say* **no**.

Keep in mind, though, that just because someone is older and wiser doesn't mean that she is stodgy and set in her ways. On the other hand, just because your CEO is a twenty-eight-year-old hipster doesn't guarantee he's going to be totally laid-back and easy to work under.

We're defining this behavior generally, **not** generationally.

SWIM-LANE FANATICS

These are big believers in not making waves. They are typically middle managers who are unlikely to be sure what they want and suffer from analysis paralysis.

They are not necessarily strong decision makers or good at sticking to their guns. They often embrace a nine-to-five mentality.

For them, work is work and life is life, and never the two shall meet. They're not looking to set the world on fire or change the status quo. However, they're easy to get along with, although not likely to challenge you.

EXAMPLE 1: THE SHEEPLE

Favorite catch phrases:

- ⏻ Case of the Mondays
- ⏻ TGIF

They are not likely to:

Stir the pot, take an aggressive stance, perform above average, ask for a raise, think outside the box.

How to get along with a Sheeple:

It's usually easy, as they're not too difficult to get along with and aren't abrasive. Take initiative yourself, and make them look good. Elevate them. This group isn't prone to taking all the credit or stealing your ideas. They are generally going to appreciate your making them and their team look good.

Be prepared to engage in small talk. Their weekends are very sacred. They want to come in and have the Monday morning "How was your weekend?" conversation and on Friday afternoon the "What are your plans?" lowdown.

Whenever you need their support on something, go to them with data and a mapped-out plan that includes a viable solution. Make it easy for them to make decisions so that they don't have to rely on their knowledge base, which is either limited or perceived as limited.

EXAMPLE 2: THE MARSHMALLOW
Favorite catch phrases:

- ⏻ **Let's chew on that**
- ⏻ **Okeydoke**

They are not likely to:

Give you direct or critical feedback, be supportive, admit they are unsure of a decision.

How to get along with a Marshmallow:

Keep encouraging them to be frank and direct with you. When they do, make sure you don't get upset, as it will prevent them from giving more constructive criticism in the future.

When they do praise you for things, particularly if it's fluffy praise, challenge them to give you more detailed feedback rather than a general response such as, "You did a really great job this week. Thanks for all your hard work."

It's unlikely they will ever leave you hanging, although they tend to care more about your liking them than being a good manager.

EXAMPLE 3: THE POLITICIAN
Favorite catch phrases:

- ⏻ My sources tell me
- ⏻ Whose side are you on?

They are not likely to:

Have competency with their responsibilities, be truthful, have close and long-term relationships, work as hard as they claim they do, keep secrets.

How to get along with a Politician:

Make them look good to peers and senior leaders. If you get credit for something, be sure to give them credit as well, being careful not to steal their thunder. Getting on their bad side is the quickest way for them to try and run you over.

The Politician is likely to be popular and charismatic and have a good pulse on how to sway senior leaders, which is a very valuable trait and something you could learn from.

But beware: You're likely to be discarded once you're no longer valuable to them. Because of that, you should be establishing relationships with other people in the organization.

SELF-PROMOTERS

Self-Promoters love to be in the spotlight. They typically have little regard for other people's schedules and assume you'll be delighted when they show up unexpectedly at your desk.

They would never let you make any decision, no matter how small, without their being involved. Forget any chance of a Self-Promoter embracing your need for more independence and less micromanagement.

Because they're overly involved with themselves, they usually fail to provide you all the information needed to complete a task and get offended when you don't ask for permission.

Self-Promoters *love* to plan and schedule meetings upon meetings before making a decision. By the time they finally decide, the golden opportunity has already passed.

EXAMPLE 1: THE CONTROL FREAK

Favorite catch phrases:

- ⏻ I wouldn't do it that way
- ⏻ Make sure you cc me

They are not likely to:

Coach you on handling a problem independently, delegate responsibility, or close the door on any opportunity as they like to have plenty of opportunity to change their minds.

How to get along with a Control Freak:

Constantly overcommunicate. Be up front with all information and give bad news first, but be quick to soften the blow with good news.

Make sure you don't take the micromanaging personally. Focus your efforts on building their trust and confidence by providing them with regular updates, and always ask permission before proceeding on anything. Because their response time tends to be slow, keep other projects moving while you're waiting for an answer.

EXAMPLE 2: THE DICTATOR

Favorite catch phrases:

- ⏻ I need it done yesterday
- ⏻ My way or the highway

They are not likely to:

Ask how you think a problem should be solved, admit to making a mistake, ever say, "Good job," let you make decisions.

How to get along with a Dictator:

Always keep them in the loop. Ask for clear instruction on how to proceed. Both will help gain their trust so that they see you as a team player. Dictators are petrified of an uprising.

Don't expect them to express confidence in you, but understand that the more you play by their rules, the more likely you are to gain their trust. If a problem arises, go to them immediately.

It's always a good idea periodically to make sure that you are both working toward the same end or that you are at least showing support of their goal.

EXAMPLE 3: THE FINGER-POINTER

Favorite catch phrases:

- ⏻ It's insurmountable
- ⏻ Someone should do something about that

They are not likely to:

Take responsibility for an issue in front of peers, complete high-level company projects, create a positive working environment, foster creativity or productive interdepartment meetings, give credit to others.

How to get along with a Finger-Pointer:

We're not going to lie: The Finger-Pointer is a dick. If you are stuck working under a person like this, keeping focused on the problem at hand rather than the toxic environment is the only thing you can do to keep your sanity.

Because they are likely to throw you and your team under the bus, get into the habit of saving all communication in the event you need to cover your butt.

Your main objective is to figure out a way to get out from under this person. Research conducted by the Center for Creative Leadership shows that trying to change your boss's mentality is a waste of time. If you're at your dream company, try to find another department that you can work in, or another manager you can work under. If you can't, it might be time to move on.

THE TEAM PLAYERS

Under this category you'll find at least one boss that you always dreamed of having. This is the group that is highly likely to encourage a subordinate's growth in addition to being proactive with their own self-development. Because of that, you don't have to be worried about anyone stealing your thunder or throwing you under the bus.

Their goal is to create a learning environment for you to test ideas. They're big on keeping promises and are there to catch you if you fall. They are supportive and focused on the entire team growing as well as the entire company growing through the actions of the team. Across the board, they demonstrate heightened leadership capabilities and attributes.

EXAMPLE 1: THE CAPTAIN
Favorite catch phrases:

- ⏻ Let's give credit where credit is due
- ⏻ My door is always open

They are not likely to:

Be disrespectful or unprofessional to an employee, take credit for something one of their team members did, shy away from tough decisions.

How to get along with a Captain:

These are the easy ones to get along with. Be eager to share your ideas.

Don't be afraid to ask for help. They would rather see that you're learning than have you wasting time trying to fumble through something.

With this type of manager, expect to be pushed—show an initiative for going above and beyond. Seek out innovative solutions, and contribute reliably. You should be striving to make them proud.

EXAMPLE 2: THE HYPER-EFFICIENT
Favorite catch phrases:

- ⏻ Take a stab at it
- ⏻ Come to me when you need help

They are not likely to:

Linger on a problem or decision, strive for perfection, waste time on formalities, niceties, or small talk, obsess over incremental gains, slow down to reevaluate enough, be overly caring/sensitive.

How to get along with a Hyper-Efficient:

Expect to be pushed and be flexible. They tend to move at the speed of light and change course on a dime.

Maintain a "done is better than perfect" attitude and call out problems ASAP. Don't sit on something or allow it to grow. As soon as you identify an issue, the Hyper-Efficient will want to know about it so that they can help create a plan to tackle it head-on.

Take both praise and criticism for what it's worth, as they tend to dole both out quickly and then move on. Thus, they are not particularly warm and fuzzy people, but they also don't hold grudges.

Be direct and to the point, and don't take the curtness to heart.

HOW TO ELEVATE YOUR BOSS WHEN YOU'RE THE STRONGER ONE

Except for superiors who fall into the Team Players category, you will encounter situations where you are stronger than your boss. However, it's still important that you remember **that person is still your boss.**

Your job isn't to undercut his or her authority. If you're smart, you'll instead strive to elevate your boss, which takes some finessing. You probably feel annoyed, thinking you must coddle and tiptoe around when all you want to do is get the job done, especially when you see an opportunity to advance your career.

Our friend Karen once had a boss who was a few years older than her, a genuine nine-to-fiver. Work was work; play was play. That lack of ambition was a problem, because the next level up for Karen was her boss's job.

There was no way for Karen to get promoted if her boss didn't get out of the way. Instead of being conniving, she made sure that her boss was aware of work she was doing with the three interns she had been charged with, especially as it pertained to practicing how to nail an interview and what they could do to improve their resume.

"Don't be afraid to ask for what you deserve," Karen would often tell them.

Soon after, her boss jokingly asked if Karen could look at her resume, too. In doing so, it opened the door for

Karen to encourage her boss, reinforcing the idea that she brought a lot of value to the company and was in a good position for a promotion.

Karen also made it a point to call out her boss's successes to other people in the company. Thus, her boss got a promotion, giving Karen the opportunity to advance as well.

Instead of working to eliminate her boss, Karen elevated her. The end was the same, but the means involved positive reinforcement—and, yes, some ass kissing.

Even if you have a prickly boss that is just a difficult person in general, most people are enthusiastic about having someone cheer them on. The key is to create teamwork and camaraderie where you're both elevating yourselves. In turn, those partnerships encourage a trust that goes both ways and leads to headway in projects and careers.

Remember, have confidence over bravado. Communicate in a way that makes it easy for your managers to make decisions, by using the tips we went over in this chapter, and be careful about presenting ideas in absolutes.

Bottom line: always strive to make your boss look good. And unless you're being asked to do something that is morally, ethically, or legally wrong, don't ever go above your boss's head unless it's a last resort.

HOW WE GOT HERE

We developed this information through by reflecting back on the managers we encountered through the years, by reading current leadership literature, and through dozens of executive and Millennial interviews. Again, the categories have nothing to do with age or experience. We know fifty-seven-year-olds who mimic the attributes of a Hyper-Efficient and twenty-six-year-olds who act like a Marshmallow. The generational gap is a lot narrower than you think.

People are what they are because we've each been exposed to different things that have shaped how we think and act. It's a waste of time and energy to try to change others or simply wish they'd just go away. Instead, think about how you can change your communication with them to achieve the best possible results.

Getting better at life includes developing a damn good understanding of the types of personalities you'll run into during your career. You need to know the cards you're playing with. In reading through these descriptions, you might have recognized yourself as one of them.

If you didn't see yourself in the "dream boss" category,

don't be offended. Instead, be proactive. Accept how some of your attributes might be perceived by others. Take responsibility, and initiate change.

When you accept that not everyone is going to approach life and work the same way you do, it's easier to see how tailoring your communication with others is what will optimize interactions and productivity.

In doing so, you sharpen your own professional-development skills. After all, the day might likely come when you're someone's boss. Be the one they'd follow into the fire, not the one they'd throw in.

CHAPTER 2 ACTION ITEMS

- ⏻ Take time to identify the leadership styles and priorities of the people you work with most.
- ⏻ Map out a plan to adapt your communication styles based on whom you're interacting with.

PART II

—

HOW TO NAVIGATE LEADERSHIP STYLES

· ·

MANAGING UP

· ·

MANAGING UP IS how you can maximize a position of growth for yourself, your boss, and the entire team.

We've identified the people that you are most likely going to encounter in the office. We've given you tools needed to communicate with them. But to successfully manage up, you must master the art of **learning** and **observing**.

Think of yourself as a sponge.

When you take the time to look at the office landscape, you will start to notice clues that reveal exactly what you're up against. As we talked about in Chapter 2, you are going to come across a cast of characters. The more time you take to understand what makes them tick, the more likely you are to find success.

It's why the first thirty to sixty days on the job are so important. Not only are you observing and learning, but it's also the most critical time for revealing your work habits and what you're going to be contributing to the organization.

But I want to make a killer impression.

We're not telling you to sit there like a drone, but while it's important to participate and show your value, it usually isn't a good idea to come in with guns blazing.

What would you consider "guns blazing?"

Recently, an executive told us of a new hire who arrived a la the Tasmanian Devil.

"We can't do it that way" and "We can't do this" were his favorite phrases, which naturally rubbed everyone the wrong way.

This guy was so rigid that he made no effort to read the room so that he could learn what the group and organizational culture was. After only thirty days, they had shuffled him to different departments and managers. He was a smart individual with the potential to be well liked, but he came in a little too hot. Although his ideas had great potential, pitching them incorrectly was his downfall.

But I've been at my job for a while now. What's left to figure out?

Just because you're not starting fresh doesn't mean you can't take some time to do more learning and observing of the people around you. If there's someone on your team you've never talked to, ask him or her to lunch. You might learn something new about that person that would help deepen your relationship or his or her contributions to the team.

The point is that it's never too late to start learning and observing, but making it a **priority** is key.

MAXIMIZE THE IMPACT OF YOUR EFFORTS

As a reader of this book, you're probably already maxing out the amount of effort you can put toward your job. Over the next few pages, we will share some next-level secrets to ensuring your hard work gets recognized for all that it's worth instead of being brushed over.

AVOID CREATING WORK FOR YOUR BOSS

Just as we talked about in chapter 1, know the answer

before you ask the question. Come armed with solutions, not just problems.

Make sure you've tried three or four or a hundred other things before going to your boss and saying, "It didn't work."

Memorize this quotation from *Steal Like an Artist*: "Google everything. And I mean *everything*. You'll either find the answer, or you'll come up with a better question."

This is so true. Googling is something that you as a Digital Native can take advantage of to prove yourself as a capable and forward-thinking employee. Fully capitalize on how much you can do on your own. Then, integrate those ideas with input from your team so that the plan of attack shows innovation as well as thoughtful collaboration.

THERE ARE NO PROBLEMS, ONLY SOLUTIONS

Simply saying, "This isn't working," or, "We have this problem," to your boss isn't enough. In the workplace, you're expected to try and solve that problem on your own. You haven't been hired to be a mindless drone. You've been hired to use your brain and your problem-solving skills. Don't just stand there and watch something burn when there's a fire extinguisher within reach.

*In the event of an actual fire, your best bet is to call 911.

KEEP IT BRIEF

Lean communication is critical to managing up. In chapter 1 we recommended you read Joseph McCormack's book, *Brief: Make a Bigger Impact by Saying Less.*

Keeping it brief pertains to written communication, everyday conversation, and pushing new or big ideas. Don't try to change everything overnight. Take initiatives one step at a time and present new options as bite-sized pieces for your managers to chew on.

When you don't agree with someone, it's always best to discuss the matter in person rather than shooting off a rambling email. Pro tip: the best email response when not agreeing with someone is simply "Let's discuss."

THE "SANDWICH TECHNIQUE" IS B.S.

This one goes for both managing up and managing down. Smashing negatives in between two positives is bullshit and doesn't work. Seriously, management school, why the hell are you teaching people this? Everyone just walks away remembering the negative stuff anyway.

When you must deliver bad news or negative feedback, just do it quickly and frankly. Ideally, add a plan for improvement.

Hopefully you're in the habit of providing good news and positive feedback regularly, so the negatives are perceived as constructive criticism rather than an ongoing attack. In any event, artificially jamming it between two compliments is not making anyone feel better.

COVER YOUR ASS (CYA)

While we're not saying to be overly paranoid that someone is out to get you at every turn, it is always helpful to keep emails and other transcribed conversations documented in case of emergency. At the very least, they can be used to help clear up a misunderstanding that might arise from a situation. Keep your defensiveness and emotions in check, though. Stay objective, and coolly and calmly present the facts as they were presented to you.

DONE IS BETTER THAN PERFECT

Mark Zuckerberg has this saying hanging in his office, and we couldn't agree more. Perfection is rarely rewarded in the corporate world; it's often much better to have something complete and almost perfect.

This doesn't mean you should produce junk, but strive for 80–90 percent right instead of 100 percent right. Most people won't notice the difference, and the time you save can be directed to another important project. (Note: If you're a doctor, pilot, or sniper, please continue to aim for 100 percent).

DO WORK THAT MATTERS

To paraphrase Lois Frankel, author of *Nice Girls Don't Get the Corner Office*, there are much better things you want to be known for than organizing the office potluck or getting the coffee.

What happens if you're always asked to do just that?

Your rehearsed deflecting skills will come in handy should you ever find yourself in that situation. When you are asked, do it, but only once. In the future, deflect by saying, "Actually, I'll mention it to the admin and see if she can take care of that for us because I want to make sure that I'm fully focused on this test/meeting."

It's not like it's beneath you, but they didn't hire you to curb everyone's caffeine fix. Even if you are the intern, still consider whether you were hired simply to fetch the coffee. Some people will say, "Yes, if they ask you to get coffee, be the best coffee-getter ever." We say screw that. Because here's a better idea: be too busy working on important projects to have time to get coffee.

DELEGATE

This is something that largely impacts women, but we also feel that it disproportionately impacts Millennials because of our self-sufficient, "I can handle this" mentality.

Let this sink in for a minute: Credit and promotions are given for **getting the job done.**

Notice it doesn't say "for doing the work." Your ability to delegate portions of a task or project is **the only thing** that will enable you to take on larger projects. Make sure you have time to focus on the hard, meaningful parts of the project that require your expertise.

SPEND THAT $$

If you're given a budget, spend it. This seems to be a somewhat Millennial phenomenon, possibly as an effect of 2008, possibly related to our own debt, but we are afraid to spend money—even when it's company money!

If you've been given a budget, your boss expects you to spend it. Unless otherwise communicated, she doesn't expect you to ask for approval on every move you make. She has her own job to do! Just don't go over budget or spend money recklessly, and you'll be fine.

If you take pride in being frugal, great. Apply it to your personal life, understanding that companies almost never reward frugality.

FAKE IT 'TIL YOU MAKE IT

Pretend to be your best even at your worst. Nobody likes a

dark cloud. Low energy just doesn't sell. Even on an awful day, if you pretend to be at your best, you're still going to be perceived much better by people. Certainly, you will seem a hell of a lot better than how you feel internally. It might take some practice, but you are fully capable of tricking your mind into believing something.

Similarly, if you don't have the expertise or every single requirement for a job, be aware of how you can compensate while quickly learning the skills you need. Women are especially guilty of passing up projects and jobs because they aren't 100 percent qualified. How can you grow if you aren't extending beyond your current skills? There are a million resources online that you can get your hands on—usually for free—that can help you expand your skill set without necessarily having to learn on the job. You can do it in your free time. It's how a lot of Millennials find themselves advancing quickly.

Seven or eight years into Rob's career, he was presented with an opportunity to open a dining and entertainment district in what was literally a hole in the ground. Up until that point, his experience had been concentrated in sports, not hospitality. But he was put on a team that was charged with making this hole in the ground one of the most profitable entertainment districts in North America.

Granted, a lot of his learning came from being tossed into the fire, but in gathering his team together and being proactive with learning more about the industry, they were able to succeed.

You can apply this to something as simple as waking up hungover on a Friday, wanting to skip the gym. Every time you quit on something, it gets easier to quit on something else. Take that headache to the gym with you and beat it up a little bit. Fake it 'til you make it.

We'll pause here to again reinforce the importance of dressing for the part, only because it's hard to fake it 'til you make it if you're wearing shorts and a T-shirt to the office.

CONFIDENCE, NOT BRAVADO

This is a big one that also goes along with guns blazing. There is such a fine line, and sometimes it's hard to pinpoint when you've crossed it.

Fundamentally, bringing everything back to yourself can be considered as bravado.

At a young age, Kate's father gave her an important pointer on this topic. They were watching a Detroit Lions football game, and Barry Sanders scored a touchdown.

"See, Kate," he said, "Barry doesn't do an end zone celebration. Because he's been there plenty of times before and will be there plenty more times. When you're successful at something, remember to act like you've been there before."

This advice stuck with Kate and has helped build her reputation as a consistent achiever. Think of the successful people you encounter in the workplace. Do they over-celebrate small feats, or do they quickly focus on getting the next big win?

When you win at life, or when you're performing well at work, act like you've been there before. Acknowledge compliments and credit with grace, share credit where due, then quickly channel the wave of energy you feel into the next project, your company, or your team.

That's confidence.

KEEP YOUR COOL WHEN YOUR BOSS UNEXPECTEDLY CALLS YOU INTO HIS OFFICE

It's rare to find anyone in corporate America who hasn't been blindsided by something that's come completely out of left field. If you do find yourself caught off guard, your best response is to **deflect** because it's important not to say anything that will put you in a bad light.

Deflect by using the following phrases:

- ⏻ "I'm going to research more into this."
- ⏻ "I'm going to put a thirty-day action plan together."
- ⏻ "Can we follow up later in the day or tomorrow morning, or have another meeting, so I can collect some more information?"

Is there a way to practice? Probably, but that's just through preparation and knowing your job, meeting with your mentors, and knowing other situations that have occurred in the office. Regardless, deflection buys you time to gather your thoughts and return armed with the information you need to make an informed decision or response.

Kate's tactic is to make sure that she completely understands the situation. When she's caught by surprise, she always reaches for a piece of paper and says, "Let me make sure that I'm getting all this information down so that I can do something about it or so that I can properly respond to it." Once she has the details, she'll ask for X amount of time to absorb the information and figure out a plan.

In a previous job, Kate was the person responsible for sending out all communications to the company's customer base. For a period of about six months, she had a feeling that her company was going to experience a big change, and not necessarily in a positive way. Then one day the CEO called her into his office. "We are getting acquired tomorrow, and I need you to send the email to our customers, but you can't tell anyone in the office about it yet." Now, it just so happened that his office was a fishbowl for the *entire* office, so not only had she been blindsided, but she also couldn't let on that anything was going wrong.

She had to quickly agree to his request knowing that the next day she'd be out of work. However, until that happened, she still had a job to do. Together, they worked out the details of what the email would contain. Because she demonstrated the ability to handle that situation professionally and calmly, afterward he went out of his way to make introductions that had job-lead potential.

In that high-stress situation, she could keep her cool because she made it a practice always to have a backup plan or next step in mind, and she knew she would land on her feet in a short amount of time.

Having the awareness of the whole picture enables you to be calmer when you are blindsided. By nature, it also makes you more receptive to change, even when that change might seem like a negative.

If you want to practice and make it fun, this is another situation where buying a car can prove to be a great learning experience. When they start throwing numbers at you, practice different ways to deflect their tactics to get what you want. Sales people are trained to put pressure on you. When we went to buy our car, numbers were being thrown out at us in rapid succession until we said, "Wait, hold on, that's not where we want to be; we'll get back you." Even though it was a high-pressure situation, deflecting gave us time to look at all the information before we committed to anything.

HOW TO BEST ENGAGE WITH OLD-SCHOOL BUSINESS TYPES

Don't lose your cool.

Seriously.

Change is very, very tough for most people, especially for this group of old-school business types. During interviews with executive coaches, a common theme revolved around the fact that at a certain age people become very secure in their life and their career and therefore extremely resistant to change. Whether it's using the latest social media app or a using cutting-edge technology, in these situations it would serve you well to present the information in bite-sized pieces. Don't push or become frustrated or hostile.

As we talked about in chapter 1, the world is a very different place than it was fifteen, twenty, and thirty years ago. Media and technology have changed, as well as the way we communicate. Be aware and respectful of the gap.

One way to present an alternative way of doing something is simply to initiate a dialogue about it. Open by saying, "This is how I usually do X. But I've noticed you do it another way. Can you tell me why you approach it your way?"

Then, zip the lip and listen.

ICYMI THEY PROBABLY WON'T GET IT

Always check your language when communicating with old-school business types. A big part of this includes avoiding the use of acronyms. More than likely, they'll have no idea what any of it means, and you don't want to turn them off or make them feel stupid.

Get into the habit of speaking plain English, not text talk.

RELATE NEW FORMS OF BUSINESS TO OLD

You can't expect seasoned managers to just sign off on the latest and greatest social media platform just because everyone else is using it. Consider the current business practice before you go into detail about what the new-school way of doing something would be. If you're trying to justify why the company needs to purchase a Facebook ad, lead with, "Here's a new way to drive this area of our business, and this is a great example of how we can do it."

To increase your odds of success, you must get a handle on what the other person already understands. Know what he or she gets excited about, and then present your idea in those terms.

For example, the CFO obviously cares about revenue numbers. So when introducing new technology that ensures correct data input, be sure to express how *you* care about revenue numbers.

RESPECT THE CULTURAL NORMS

If you have a job interview or a meeting with somebody who is a suit wearer, put a blazer on.

If someone wants you to take off your shoes when you enter his or her office, take them off.

Therefore, it's so important to be always **learning** and **observing.** Pick up on those little cues. They serve as clues for what's important to that person. Then, adapt as best you can to demonstrate your respect for the cultural norm. It's one more way to build trust.

PLAY TO YOUR AUDIENCE

Early in his career, our friend Damian made the cardinal mistake of coming in with guns blazing.

He came off as a cold Hyper-Efficient. He always put the tasks at hand before the niceties. Sure, there were some quick high fives and attaboys, but he was failing at being a good manager, to the point where his team wasn't performing at an optimal level.

Part of the problem was his lack of emotional intelligence at the time. He didn't have enough empathy to understand how social awareness and relationship management come into play at the office.

He was doing his job and assumed that alone was enough to make him, and his team, succeed. But he was "me-focused" and lost sight of how self-awareness and self-management are very tied into social awareness and relationship management. If he had been more aware, he would have quickly keyed into the fact that some of his team needed a little bit more of the warm and fuzzy to succeed.

Thinking back to our training as athletes, there was so much emphasis on controlling your emotions to stay focused. If you aren't in control of your emotions, and you have these ups and downs, then you end up overthinking a lot of situations and expending a lot of energy on things that aren't productive, which is not good for your physical or mental health.

Lacking emotional intelligence is very stressful and can wear on you.

Try to keep your emotions consistent from day to day. It doesn't just make you more likable and help your relationships. It also helps you physically make sure that you're dedicating your efforts to productive stress, not unproductive stress.

It's all part of learning how to successfully manage up. To quote Chinese philosopher Lao Tzu: *"Knowing others is intelligence; knowing yourself is true wisdom. Mastering others is strength; mastering yourself is true power."*

CHAPTER 3 ACTION ITEMS

- ⏻ Think back to the past week. What percent of the time were you doing work that matters? Plan to delegate or deflect more of the low-value work next week.
- ⏻ Find someone at your company outside your department that can be your ally. Start developing these relationships.
- ⏻ Practice brevity. Start with making your emails as succinct as possible.

CHAPTER 4

. . . .

IDEA ADVANCEMENT

. . . .

WHEN IT COMES to a new idea, people inherently either love it or hate it. As we've talked about over the previous chapters, the tendency to move toward or away from something is typically the result of experience, industry, generations, and geographic regions.

This is where the foundation from chapter 1 comes in to play. That's your armor, and now you're ready for battle.

HOW TO GET PEOPLE TO EMBRACE YOUR IDEA

Typically, when someone wants to advance an idea, they embrace one of the following two strategies.

1. SHOWCASE POTENTIAL RESULTS

The move is incentivized by giving people something more than what they currently have or think they need, especially if they see others benefiting from it. It taps into that *"I want what the cool kids have"* mentality.

When Kate was hoping to get her company to embrace a certain new technology, she first reached out to people she knew who were already using it. Because of those conversations, she created mini case studies showing actual results that could be presented to the powers that be.

2. HIGHLIGHT VULNERABILITIES

This is done to move away from the status quo. It's one of those *"If we don't change, then here are some negative possible consequences"* talks.

We know a girl named Regina who was trying to get her organization to see the value in backing up all their files on the cloud, just in case their server went down. This was a concern she had brought up repeatedly. However, either no one understood it, or nobody ever considered the real possibility of a server crash—until it happened. Thus, the company lost around $90,000 in a matter of hours.

REMEMBER: THE INTERNET IS SCARY TO A LOT OF PEOPLE

Although the Internet has evolved dramatically, as well

as the way we can do business with it, many companies have been slow to embrace it. Make sure you keep this in mind when putting together your pitch.

Television, radio, newspapers—many senior leaders just can't seem to let these go. They're used to how things have been done for the past twenty, thirty, even forty years and are struggling to embrace a new model.

That's understandable.

We as a generation are still infatuated with the slap bracelet, which hasn't been around since the nineties.

We have something in common with the old guard: an appreciation and affinity for something we grew attached to through repeated exposure and usage. Call it nostalgia, but we all experience it in many ways with many different things.

Simply put: It's hard to say good-bye to yesterday, especially as it pertains to technology. Technology can be very intimidating and weird to people who aren't used to using it.

It's not enough to extol the virtues of digital technology and expect everyone at the office to jump on the bandwagon with you, no questions asked.

Learn to manage up across multiple bosses by always staying aware of the fact that the best deals in partnership and communication include a win-win-win for all involved.

Throughout your career, you will discover that your middle managers and executive leaders often have two different agendas. It's up to you in this growth stage to diplomatically manage them fairly and squarely.

Kate's work spans marketing and sales, departments whose relationships have historically been particularly contentious. This is often because marketing typically looks six months to a year down the road, while sales wants to close the deal yesterday.

Within that framework, there's also a competition for budgets. There's a finite amount of money available, and everyone wants it.

A staple point of her job is to identify technology tools that benefit both teams.

When she does, she changes her presentation of the material based on who she is talking to. The points she makes to the marketing team are different from those she highlights for sales or finance people. By tailoring her talking points to prove how a tool will benefit each division, she also reinforces the benefit that the entire company will receive. Thus, the process is a collaboration, rather than a win-lose.

IS THE INTERNET A FAD?

"Well, this Internet thing, it's probably just a fad that's going to pass."

It was early on in Rob's career when he heard those words escape from the lips of a senior manager. It was during a strategy meeting about whether to implement a basic email marketing system. The company wanted to bolster ticket sales through an e-newsletter that would be distributed to their client base.

He sat down at the massive conference table that day feeling shiny and bright. The world hadn't ended with Y2K. Life had gone on without needing life support from a frantically-purchased generator, and digital technology was unfolding as a way to reach target audiences better and faster than ever before.

He was eager, ready! But those thirteen words made him realize that as far as the room was concerned, he was just a kid who had somehow snuck a seat at the adult-only table.

Hindsight makes it easy for us all to smile knowingly at

each other. *A fad? What a dumb thing to say!*

However, the idea that Internet technologies are just a fad has come up repeatedly over the course of our careers. As two Millennial MBAs with strong marketing backgrounds in technology as well as sports and entertainment, we've heard the same thing said about securing domain names and social media feeds. There have been encounters with more furrowed brows, more skepticism. "What's the point? It's probably just a fad."

As Digital Natives, we've seen how corporate America tends to easily dismiss the importance of investing in critical areas of digital technology. It happened so many times that it made us wonder, *Do some of these people seriously think* the Internet *is a fad?*

When you're a young professional entering an arena with people who have decades worth of experience doing certain things a certain way, the mere mention of change can put you in the center of a minefield. Getting your ideas through can seem like an impossible-to-achieve fairy tale. When a company does check a new technology off the list, they're usually slow to put the resources behind it.

"We need to have a Facebook page," your boss finally agrees. "Let the intern run it."

Sound familiar?

When you find yourself in such a situation, you must realize that it's not necessarily a generational thing. It's most likely a communication thing.

Remember, these people who are wary of your ideas were also once in your shoes. There was a time when they had to argue the benefits of television advertising over radio or print. As we've talked about, your job entails learning how to make the new digital landscape more relatable to colleagues who weren't raised on it like we Digital Natives were. Again, you'll generate more successful results by paying close attention to what makes them tick.

HOW TO ADVANCE YOUR IDEA

Whether you showcase results or highlight potential vulnerabilities, at some point you're going to have to pitch your idea to advance your own agenda. Advancing your agenda is advancing your idea. However, a lot of people are afraid to even make the ask to get their idea approved.

But not you! You've been armed with all the fundamentals of the past chapters to put you in the right position to know how to talk to the right person in a way that will resonate most positively with them.

THE PITCH METHOD

Because of great successes and a few face-plants, here's what we've found works best for getting people to run toward, rather than away from, your ideas. We put together the "PITCH Method" to help, and who doesn't like a relevant acronym?

PREP

We've already talked about researching, but focus on the outcomes when arguing your case, particularly with technology. Technology, specifically, is native to you but probably is not native to your audience, so you're leading with a problem. Your opinion is not enough; you've got to leverage your idea by proving what the data shows and how your strategy answers the need. Be careful not to just throw data at someone; it'd be like using Chinese to communicate with someone who doesn't speak that language. Make sure that you take data and turn it into insights.

Also, don't shy away from including negative data. Often, that negative data is the most useful. It shows you where the problems or weaknesses are. While it might seem to reflect poorly on you, it gives you a clearer course for the future.

Recently, Kate looked back at her company's blog growth numbers and noticed that they were stagnating. Instead of hiding that information in her report, she called it out. In doing so, they discovered a broken link and could fix the problem.

INSPECT

This is where you look at it yourself. Make sure that your data, what you've prepped for, is accurate. Fill in any gaps. Play devil's advocate yourself, and plan to address the objections you come up with head-on.

Make sure it flows and that the pieces are in an order that makes sense. Aim to get to the meat of the idea within the first five minutes before your audience has a chance to be distracted. Eliminate any points that do not add value to the specific audience.

TALK

Everybody's going to have a different opinion, and some of those might never have dawned on you. Talking things through with someone you trust is critical. They'll bring an argument that you may have missed while you were doing your own inspecting. It's a great way to decrease the odds of being blindsided during your pitch.

CONSOLIDATE

Your pitch needs to be concise, or it's not going to be heard. Tighten it up, and remove any unnecessary filler. Challenge yourself to remove as many words as you can from a sentence and still keep your point intact.

HOOK

Finish the presentation with a memorable impression. Make sure you hook your audience by saying: *"And this is how we're going to make a million dollars. This is how we can improve X percent."* Keep the description of the benefits relevant to the business that you're talking about.

TIPS ON HOW TO NAIL THE PITCH

Most of this you've picked up over the past few chapters, but it's important to reiterate again because it all relates to how you can nail a pitch.

1. Read the room. Know who your audience is and what tone they'll respond best to.

2. Speak on their level. Use terminology they will understand or that you can easily explain.

3. Dress for the part. Wear something professional that you feel comfortable and confident in. You don't want to be fidgeting with an ill-fitting garment.

4. Be aware of your body language. Crossed arms come off as defensive and closed-off, even if you're not.

5. If you are using any kind of computer or technology, expect it to fail. Have a backup, but also be able to pitch your idea without it.

6. Liven things up. Instead of PowerPoint, use Prezi to create an animated presentation. You have the floor, and the stage is yours. This is an awesome opportunity to set yourself apart from the crowd.

7. Do a couple of practice runs so you are overly prepared and extremely familiar with the information. You don't want to appear robotic or give off that "deer in the headlights" vibe. Remember that old quotation, *"Luck is what happens when preparation meets opportunity."*

8. Don't overwhelm. Allow your audience to chew on bite-sized chunks before trying to change everything overnight.

9. Be respectful of people's time and aware that key players might have to duck out early due to other obligations. For this reason, it's critical to get to the point quickly, before anyone has a chance to get distracted. Unlike in school, you're almost never penalized for a presentation ending early.

10. Understand the roles that everyone in the room plays in making the decision. Most likely, it will include influencers and implementers. Realize that some traditional methodologies might be disrupted by the decision. Be mindful that change can be intimidating and scary to the people tasked with putting your idea into action.

When we've failed to make the pitch, often it was because we led off with the wrong thing. In doing so, we turned the room off completely, or it didn't engage everyone in our audience.

Success has come when we've taken the time to implement all the above techniques and, especially, when we used a personalized touch.

During a particularly contentious pitch for the new entertainment and dining district project Rob was working on, he kept his presentation as concise as humanly possible. For his hook, he told everyone to look under their chairs. When they did, they found a gift card for a free beer at a new business that would be opening on the site.

It was his "Oprah" moment. *Everyone in the audience gets a new car!*

It worked because, going into it, he knew damn well that no one wanted to be there. There had been no budget for lunch, and that made everyone even crabbier. The gift cards were a way for him to creatively engage his audience and thank them for their time. It was a tension reliever and made a memorable, positive impression.

CHAPTER 4 ACTION ITEMS

- ⏻ Print out the steps to the PITCH method to have them as a reminder for your next ask.
- ⏻ When you encounter pushback, ask questions and listen to find the real reason for resistance.

CHAPTER 5

. . . .

CAREER ADVANCEMENT

. . . .

A KEY COMPONENT to career advancement is making sure that you are constantly learning and building relationships so that you are ready for when those golden opportunities come your way.

Because let's face it: Often people don't just wake up one day and say, "I'm going to get a new job," or, "I need a promotion." It's more of a slow burn that can take years of planning.

When you actively dedicate time to learning and observing as we talked about in the previous chapter, you prepare yourself for the next level even before it's time for you to make that leap.

Finding yourself in a situation where you realize, *Oh, hell. I need a new job like yesterday*, is rarely beneficial. Being backed against a wall fosters a breeding ground of knee-jerk, desperate decision making that can keep you on a mediocre path.

Remember: By the time you need a favor, it's too late to build the relationship.

WHERE TO START

Getting out of your comfort zone is, well, uncomfortable. No matter whether you're just starting out as an intern or have ten years of killer experience under your belt, making the leap can be unsettling and filled with second-guessing. Therefore, it's important to develop a support system early on, people that you'll feel at ease talking to about your concerns. Mentors, advocates—call them what you want, but they're the ones you can rely on to talk you down from the ledge.

Rob has a couple of people in his organization who aren't even in his department or line of work whom he regularly bounces ideas off of. Those individuals have become helpful in situations where there has been an opportunity to grow, to improve a certain aspect of a project, or to get involved with a high-level one. They also know where the bodies are buried, and what projects are toxic.

It's important that you realize those lifelines won't just materialize out of nowhere. You should actively seek them out. As we discussed in chapter 1, LinkedIn is one of the greatest networking resources you have at your fingertips. Identify people in the industry, whether they work at your company or not, and add them to your digital rolodex.

You've got to be comfortable with making the ask, though. If the very thought of reaching out to someone makes you nervous, consider whether your organization offers peer-to-peer networking events, or find a volunteer opportunity either internally or externally. Force yourself to get comfortable interacting with people and activities that fall outside of your little circle. You'll learn from those experiences and get better at them with each swing, particularly if you are not somebody who is overly outspoken to begin with.

Kate's friend Cady does a lot of pro-bono consulting because she doesn't feel quite comfortable yet with the idea of charging people for her time or the advice she's giving them, since she's still a younger professional. But by doing so, she's created a network and proactively taken small steps out of her comfort zone, just by reaching out to strangers and starting a conversation. Both actions will eventually enable her to make a leap when an opportunity comes along.

Rob once volunteered to give a keynote address at an industry-specific event just to sharpen his public-speaking skills.

Writing this book is another example of getting out of our comfort zones. Sometimes we feel like complete idiots, worrying that our points aren't getting across. We get on a good roll, and then suddenly it comes to a screeching halt. *What the hell were we trying to say there?* We push through it, though, and we're learning as we go.

Think about it this way: People who want to run in a marathon don't just wake up one day and pound the pavement for twenty-six miles, do they? Of course not. They build their endurance with regular training.

BUILDING NEW CONNECTIONS

As awkward as it might feel to initiate a conversation with someone you don't know that well, there are things you can do to ease the pain.

If you're worried about someone slamming the phone down on you, don't be. Not once have we ever reached out to somebody for coffee or a five-minute conversation and had him or her say no. Generally, people are willing to help you if you ask in the right, courteous way.

So, what do we mean by that?

EVALUATE BEFORE YOU EMAIL

Don't email people on Monday morning or Friday afternoon. Nobody wants another message clogging up their inbox at those points in time. Instead, email them when you know they are at lunch, taking into consideration what time zone they're in. A lot of professionals tend to catch up on emails on Sunday night before they go into the office. We've had good success sending emails at 9:00 p.m. on a Sunday night. Their kids are already in bed, and they are just getting ready for the week ahead—hopefully with a glass of wine in their hand.

KEEP IT SHORT AND SWEET

We employ a rule where we try not to send an email that won't fit on a mobile screen. Practice by typing up an email and sending it to yourself. If it fits within your mobile screen, then you're good. If somebody has to scroll down for the nugget of information, you are putting yourself in the danger zone. The first email should contain a couple of direct sentences about what you're after and ask how the recipient prefers to receive more information. If she says email, then you can send a longer note. Sending someone a two-page message right from the get-go is going to overwhelm her. She'll take one look and mentally file it as something she can respond to or read later. Then she'll forget about it. The best way to get your information across is to make it quick and snackable. Also, before you hit send, be sure to check your grammar and spelling. Then, check it again just to be sure.

MAKE IT EASY

You should make it easy for the another person to connect with you. We've found it's helpful to include specific time frames on a handful of dates rather than unlimited options. If you are meeting someone in person, take the time to find out where he is located and suggest a coffee shop that's across the street from his office. Make it super convenient for him to give you just a little chunk of his time.

BUILDING YOUR OFFICE REPUTATION

There are many subtle things you can do in the workplace that will impact your perceived capability. These things are essential to establishing a positive reputation among your coworkers and superiors.

A SEAT AT THE TABLE

In her book, *Lean In*, Sheryl Sandberg emphasizes how important it is for women to claim their seat at the table, rather than being courteous and taking a side chair. We agree. In general, if you were invited to the meeting, you're important enough to have a seat at the table.

Take this one step further though: Try to sit next to the most powerful person in the room. This has two benefits:

1. You'll have an opportunity for face time and casual conversation with him or her (just make sure you remember the conversation tips from chapter 1).

2. Some of his or her power will magically transfer to you. It's like you get to be part of his or her power force field for a while. Others in the room will notice that you are not afraid of power and will unconsciously attribute more power to you.

EARNING TRUST DESPITE YOUR AGE

While still in his thirties, Kate's former college professor Neil Sullivan ended up scoring a gig as the Athletic Director at the University of Dayton. It was a huge accomplishment for someone of his relatively young age.

We reached out to Neil to ask for his recipe for success. His response:

"I bet my career on people and organizational culture. The most important action I took to accelerate my career was working with and for people whom I admire personally and professionally. The culture of my employer and the leadership led to the pace of acceleration."

We pushed further for an understanding of the challenges he might face regularly being the youngest person in a room full of important people. Neil again pointed back to the foundation and relationships he'd established, well before accepting his position:

"I'm often the youngest person in the room, but I never make an issue of my age. I believe the best way to earn trust is to deliver. Competence, hard work, sound judgement, ethics, and good working relationships with people transcend age and demographics. It's all about results and relationships. You have to have both, and trust comes from those."

This is some powerful stuff. Neil paints a clear picture that while skills and knowledge are important to the development process, the trust comes once you've built a solid foundation of measurable results combined with strong working relationships. That trust is key to your advancement.

WATCH OUT FOR THE TECHNOLOGY TIME SUCK

While it's easy to get drunk on all that power we have at the click of a mouse, it's equally as easy to become totally entranced. We have so much more available to us than ever before, especially when it comes to entertainment options.

As we all know, these entertainment sources tend to become black holes. The trick to avoid getting lost in one is to give yourself time limits. Allocate fifteen minutes for Instagram, one hour for television—whatever the case may be. Tailor your social media feeds to be a little less Kardashian and a little more business related. Use Google news or a similar aggregator to skim for topics that you might have a little interest in and that will enrich your knowledge base or, as we talked about in chapter 1, serve as conversation starters with other people.

According to "Measuring Trends in Leisure: The Allocation of Time over Five Decades" by Mark Aguiar and Erik Hurst, since 1965 there has been a roughly five-hour weekly increase in leisure time for the average worker aged twenty-one to sixty-five. So, what are we doing with all our additional free time?

Watching television.

Our efficiencies have improved tremendously, yet we're spending all this leisure time passively watching mindless television and filling our heads with crap. You burn more calories when you are sleeping than you do when you are watching TV. Have you noticed that TV even gives you a false sense of productivity? "Yes! I planned to watch the premiere of this show tonight, right on time, and I did!

Check that off the list!" Or, "Wow, I finished the entire six seasons!" Admit it, TV viewing has made you feel productive. But what does it get you?

We're suggesting you consider just how much time you spend watching TV, and how much of that you could dedicate to other enjoyable endeavors.

If you love messing around on Photoshop, take an online course and use it to sharpen your skills, or better yet, get Adobe certified. If you find yourself obsessively taking photos of your food, start a blog. Being productive doesn't have to be boring, and if you're smart about it, you can capitalize on ways to make it work for you.

FINDING THE SPARK

Voltaire wrote: *"One day everything will be well, that is our hope. Everything's fine today, that is our illusion."*

We get it: The job you have now with the flexible schedule, casual dress code, fun coworkers, and free food is comfortable. You're relatively good at it and making decent money. But ask yourself: Are you living up to your potential? Will you be happy if you're still doing the same thing in ten, or even five years? If the answer is no, the time to act is now.

AVOID BEING YOUR OWN ROADBLOCK

It takes a little bit of a reflection to figure out if the person standing in your way is the same one you see in the mirror every day.

Feeling as if you're unhireable is a huge issue for Digital Natives fresh out of college or in their early twenties. They tend to read every single bullet on a job description and say, "Well, I can do forty-eight of these fifty bullets, but there are two on here that I can't do, so I'm not qualified for this job," or, "This job says that it requires five years of experience, and I only have three, so what's the point of applying?"

Over the past few years, we've sent our friend Kevin about fifteen jobs that he would be great at, but every time his response is the same: "Yeah, I'll apply, but first I need to get better at this," or, "First I need to do this," or, "First I need to make my resume look better."

That's a lot of "firsts" standing in the way. Each has ensured he's missed out on many potential opportunities. (Hell, some of them we even had a connection to and knew he had a good shot!) As we talked about before, it's a waste of time to sit around and wait for the perfect job. Instead, be proactive and close the gap by teaching yourself the skills that are missing.

If it comes up in the interview, address it head-on and say, "That's an area I don't have direct experience with, but here is how I plan to make up for it by learning what I need to be successful at this job. Plus, these other skills I have will help me pick it up right away." Rely on your Digital Native superpowers to research the job properly so you're not coming in empty-handed.

A friend of ours enjoys public speaking so much that she officiates weddings on the side. It's something that makes her stand out from the crowd. Not many interviewers easily forget someone who provides such a concrete example of how she is proactively sharpening her skill set. Plus, although it's not a bullet she can put on her resume under her current job responsibilities, it's something that she can use as leverage when applying for one that requires public-speaking experience. Don't be afraid to pull things from outside your career and your personal life that can help you stand out in a positive way.

Remember, most job descriptions at large companies are usually written by the HR department, which typically doesn't have a great sense of what's truly required of the position or the culture of the team.

Instead of ruling yourself out for a job, wait until somebody else tells you, "No, you are not a fit." If you don't try, the answer is always no.

The point we're trying to make is that you're going to have enough hurdles to overcome in life. Don't make yourself one of them.

BUT MY CURRENT JOB IS SO COMFORTABLE

Another common theme we hear among our peers has to do with getting too comfortable in their jobs. You know what we're talking about, the "Oh, I'll probably start looking for a new job sometime in the future" people.

Listen, time flies. In the blink of an eye your tomorrow will be your yesterday. It's easy to get complacent, but guess what? Before you know it, six years will have gone by, and when that happens, are you going to be satisfied doing the same thing for the same rate of pay that you are today?

Besides the fact that you'll probably regret becoming dormant, your resume isn't going to look so great if you aren't showing some sort of advancement. Plus, a potential employer could read that as a lack of initiative on your part.

Mountain climber and leadership consultant Alison Levine has said, "Fear is okay; complacency is what will kill you." This is coming from a woman who has scaled Mt. Everest more than once. No matter what mountain you are climbing, figuratively or literally, you have to be able to act and react quickly in an environment that is constantly changing.

Complacency is one of the biggest dangers no matter what the generation, but Millennials are particularly susceptible. This is mainly because we're told that everyone is doing everything at a later age. "Fifty is the new thirty" and all that jazz. We're told that it's okay to go after your dream job when you're thirty rather than right now. So, we get lazy because, hey, thirty is a long way off, right?

You also should keep in mind what we said about it taking months, even years, to find a new job that's a good fit.

Or maybe you come out of college not exactly knowing what you want to do, or you aren't that interested in the jobs that come with your degree. When that happens, we sometimes feel like failures, uncomfortable with switching directions after investing all our time with one specific goal in sight. It's okay to change course, though, and it's totally normal to change what you want your career path to look like as you grow. The more life you experience, the more experiences you will have that can translate into applicable skills for a new career course. Technology has revolutionized the way we can develop and transform our skills, making it much more feasible and realistic to switch career paths.

HOW TO NEGOTIATE A BIGGER PAYCHECK

There is no getting around it. This is an uncomfortable conversation, especially for women—which is why it's so important to plan what you're going to say, talk it through, and script it, as we discussed in the last chapter. Deploy the PITCH method! If applicable, enlist the help of somebody to practice with. It will make you a lot more comfortable and confident with the actual act of making the ask, critical components to successful negotiation.

Kate likes to write out word for word exactly what she would say—super bullet points, if you will. Then, she repeats it back to herself and can see how something might not come off right. She also tries to anticipate every potential response to make sure she's not blindsided. *If I say this and then they argue back with that, what's my move going to be?*

Mentors can be valuable with helping you think through this. They've been in the same position before and can share their own experiences.

THOSE DAMN MILLENNIALS—THEY'RE SO ENTITLED

Millennials have gotten a reputation as having a sense of entitlement when it comes to asking for a promotion or trying to climb the ladder as quickly as possible without having "paid our dues."

We once heard of a private financial management group that had a strict, five-year track that young associates had to complete before they were promoted to an advisor role. One of the employees was a Millennial who often spent time out of the office working on projects during evenings and weekends. When she asked for a promotion two years into her tenure there, the boss said no. "You haven't paid your dues" was the response. "Plus, what would the clients say if I sent a twenty-five-year-old into the room?" Frustrated and feeling undervalued, she quit.

In her boss's mind, she came off as an entitled brat because he didn't count the off-hours she was working toward their set-in-stone, five-year track. In this situation, it isn't a matter of who was right and who was wrong because, clearly, there was a communication breakdown on both sides. Instead of assuming he knew how hard she was working off the clock, she should have taken the initiative to articulate it in a professional, positive light.

She also should have probed a bit further into the five-year-track rule and initiated regular meetings to find out if there were different ways she could exceed expectations to advance to the next level in a shorter amount of time. To combat any issues of ageism, she could have tried to appear more mature at work in what she wore. We've often used glasses to appear more tenured. You might think it's crazy, but remember, perception is reality. If you want to be viewed as a seasoned pro, dress and talk like one. Shatter all notions that you're too young to represent the company or meet with clients by presenting yourself as a mature professional.

What ultimately sucks in this situation is that the company lost a go-getter of an employee because neither party navigated the communication divide effectively.

We're not saying it's pointless to work during the off-hours, but maintaining visible presence goes a long way with the old-school types. Even if you work from home, make tiny efforts to show yourself. Answer emails in a timely fashion or initiate thoughtful participation in the latest Slack discussion that's relevant to your boss.

Proving you are a team player will help combat a lot of this, too. Lend a hand when a coworker needs help, or offer to volunteer on a project outside of your department. Demonstrate how you've consistently gone above and beyond in a way that advances the whole team or company, rather than just yourself, in order for your superiors to feel your request for a promotion or pay raise is justified. Google best-selling author Ramit Sethi's briefcase technique for some practical tips on how to effectively demonstrate your value.

It's always important to put your request for a raise or promotion in terms of what value you bring as it relates to your job, not what you need for your personal life. It doesn't matter that money is tight at home. That is not the point. The point is the optimum value that you do, and will, bring to the company.

Also, before you ask for benefits beyond the norm—such as permission to work from home when it's not standard at the company, requesting a standing desk when no one else has one, or asking to leave early on Thursdays for softball practice—understand that you are more likely to get a green light if you've already proven yourself to be reliable and indispensable.

You can always ask for the benefit on a trial basis if your boss is hesitating to say yes.

BUT I'M DOING EVERYTHING I'M SUPPOSED TO DO!

Congresswoman Lois Frankel hits it home with this one: "Doing everything you're supposed to do isn't being pro-active. It's only doing what you're supposed to."

Hard work alone is rarely enough to get you promoted. Lois emphasizes that likability, strategic thinking, net-working, and being a team player are some of the other factors that impact your perceived qualifications. It under-scores the value in building relationships.

WHEN YOU GET A PROMOTION, ASK WHAT IT INCLUDES

Too many times we've heard a friend say, "Great news, I got promoted at work!" only to have him or her follow it up with a wishy-washy description of what has changed.

Think of a promotion as a new job. You should get a revised set of expectations and responsibilities from your boss (or new boss) that you both agree on, as well as a new compensation plan that includes any additional perks you're set to receive.

What's that? The promotion doesn't include a raise?

This is always a tough one. We are firm believers that a title change also warrants a compensation change, but understand that there are special circumstances. Again, think about the promotion as a new job. Would you accept the new job if it paid exactly what you are already making? If so, then maybe this is okay. Just make sure that "special circumstance" isn't you being a pushover or a chicken to ask.

THE IMPORTANCE OF FINDING MENTORS

"If it doesn't go both ways, then it's not mentoring."

That's how Kate's mentor KC sums up the ideal scenario. In other words, it's not a mentor relationship unless both people are benefitting from it in a substantial way.

THE BUDDY SYSTEM

Having a mentor means you don't have to go it alone. It gives you somebody to bounce your ideas off of and get honest, trustworthy feedback back from.

You can't call your mom and say, "Hey, does this sound like a fair salary to you?" because your mom is going to say, "Of course. Honey, you are the most valuable person *ever*."

Ask the same question of your mentor, and he or she might say, "Probably a little high," or, "No, you should definitely ask for more."

Kate asked Felice, one of her mentors who spent forty-five years working at a major financial firm, for her perspective on the topic of women-specific challenges in the workplace. "I don't really see being a female as a disadvantage, just a different challenge. There are studies that show women are better in finance because they are more empathetic than men. Women do have to work harder and want it more in order to balance it with everything else, but that usually results in more success."

WHERE TO START

Ask your current corporation if they have any mentoring programs you can join. Check with your human resources or your company leaders and see what is available for you to take advantage of. Start scouring LinkedIn and make some connections. Again, use a mentor search to step out of your comfort zone to help build your confidence.

DECIDE WHO YOU WANT TO BECOME

Kate's mentor KC recommends that you should decide who you want to become, find the person that has the job that you want to have in the future, and then do everything you can to learn alongside that person. You're not looking to clone someone. You're looking for someone who has blazed a path. Rather than simply following them, integrate their tips into your own skill set so that you can blaze your own.

DOES AGE MATTER?

It's not age that makes someone a good mentor; it's experience. We could be mentors to somebody older than us that was coming into our field. There are some senior executives that we've worked with over the years who will ask to meet regularly with us to talk about what's trending in our field.

There are plenty of opportunities for us Millennials to be technology mentors for older generations.

Listen, you're not Cinderella, and your mentor isn't holding a perfectly sized glass slipper. An ideal match is usually when one person sees the same strengths in the other. Notice we said *strengths*, not *perspective*. As we talked about in chapter 2, being able to understand and empathize with the other point of view will only help you grow and succeed in the business world.

KC has twenty years more experience in the industry than Kate, has seen a lot more changes, and is more developed in her interactions with other people. However, Kate has the perspective of being a Digital Native with a different way of thinking about the technology tools that they both use on the job.

A mentor isn't somebody who will take you under your wing and show you every little thing you need to know. A mentor is someone you can proactively learn from, while also providing him or her value in return. Sometimes those relationships are very hard to find. People who can make the right connections for you or help you navigate a couple of roadblocks at work based on their own experiences also make for great mentors.

Don't have this ridiculous view that your mentor is going to be "the One" who fulfills your every need while also grooming you for the next big thing. That's a fairy tale.

Even better than a mentor? Advocates. An advocate is someone in a position of power that can actually promote you or advocate for you in some way. Seek out these people, too—they are the gateway to fast advancement.

You need to have different mentors for different things, too. The person who makes a good work mentor might not be the one you turn to for guidance on how to live a healthier lifestyle.

MAKE ALLIES, NOT ENEMIES

Although this can be advantageous to everyone, it's generally something that is critical for women.

If you promote yourself or your strengths too much, it's generally seen as aggressive behavior. It tends to turn people off and get you labeled as a bitch.

It shouldn't, but that's the reality.

To combat that mentality, a good strategy is to find other allies on your team that promote you and in turn you promote them. If you see someone not getting credit for a project he or she worked hard on, make sure you employ some "amplification" to bring it to people's attention.

According to the *Washington Post*, "Women in the White House started using a simple rhetorical technique to stop interruptions and reinforce points made by other women. When a woman made a good point, another woman would repeat it, and give credit to the originator. This made the idea harder to ignore, or to steal. The women called the technique 'amplification.'"

DON'T JUST DROP THE MIC

When you do find another job, always try to give your current employer at least two weeks' notice that you are leaving. Also, aim for spending a full year with a company before moving on. It looks better on your resume and to future employers, but also a lot can change in a year. You might end up in a better spot or with a new boss, or simply have more time to ensure the next move is a really good fit and not just "something better."

CHAPTER 5 ACTION ITEMS

- ⏻ Sit at the table in this week's big meeting. Ideally, sit next to the most powerful person in the room.
- ⏻ Evaluate whether you are satisfied and being compensated fairly in your current role. If not, plan to change that ASAP. If so, start planning for your next step early.
- ⏻ Make a list of anyone you could call a mentor. Then plan to either nurture them or to expand that list.
- ⏻ Design a system for nurturing your network. Aim for two email outreaches per week to people you've identified as important, and build from there.

PART III
—
HOW TO LEVEL UP

CHAPTER 6

. . . .

ALWAYS BE LEARNING

. . . .

A COMMON SAYING that Martha Stewart likes to use is "When you're through changing, you're through."

It's more important than ever to always be learning. In fact, it's critical.

Why? Because although many jobs are starting to become automated, learning has a track record of beating advances in technology.

Great, I'm being replaced by a computer. So what the hell is the point of learning?

Technology is awesome, but if no one knows how to sell

it, teach it, and use it, what's the point?

As *Dilbert* creator Scott Adams likes to say, "Every skill you acquire doubles your odds of success."

Business, and life in general, is more dynamic and fast-paced these days. If you rest on your laurels even for a second, you risk getting left behind in the dust.

I feel as if I'm the only one in the room who's not an expert.

Sometimes it may feel as if everybody else in the office knows more than you do. That's not necessarily true. It's just that they know different things based on their own experiences. Everyone brings a unique skill set to the table. What's important is that you always make learning a priority.

Your superiors and more seasoned coworkers weren't born with an expert knowledge of how everything in the office works. Imagine how everyone felt when computers started replacing typewriters, and then when email started replacing fax machines. People had to take the time to figure it out, feeling like complete idiots until they did. So don't get discouraged. Everyone has been in the same shoes at some point in their careers.

THE DIFFERENCE BETWEEN SKILLS AND KNOWLEDGE

Remember the quotation from Chinese philosopher Lao Tzu that we talked about?

"Knowing others is intelligence; knowing yourself is true wisdom. Mastering others is strength; mastering yourself is true power."

If you have a better self-awareness of where you fit among the personality types we discussed in chapter 2, it's going to make you better equipped to address your weak spots.

As we mentioned, Kate's not particularly talented with soft skills—that is, the warm and fuzzy. She's never going to be the person who is running up to give you a hug or dying to hold your baby. However, what's important is her ability to adapt to situations that she doesn't necessarily favor and handle them with grace regardless.

Does this take practice and preparation? You bet. The key is being warm and polite, without compromising your authenticity.

When you are invited on the spot to an event you have no interest in attending, practice this reply: "Oh, that's so nice of you to include me!" (Notice that you can compliment them without lying that the event sounds fun.) "I'll have to check my schedule." (This buys you time to come up with another pleasant decline, or for them to just forget about inviting you.) Then stop. Don't elaborate further, or you will find yourself veering toward the inauthentic again.

If you know your personality and are aware of your weak spots, it enables you to compensate for them in other areas.

DON'T EVER STOP GROWING

In his book *The 15 Invaluable Laws of Growth,* author John Maxwell says, "Growth stops when you lose tension between where you are and where you could be."

Skills and knowledge are things you can always gain or adapt so that you can progress, and neither is limited only to your successes. Go out there and get your hands dirty. Don't worry about falling flat on your face. If it happens, so what? At least you tried, and frankly, often it's through our failures that we discover the most useful tools for success.

As Nelson Mandela once said, "I never lose. I either win or I learn."

Begin by taking inventory. Identify what skills you currently have and what you are interested in learning. Then, slow your roll. Don't assume that within a year of being hired you already learned everything you can possibly know about doing your job.

Pop psychology writer Malcolm Gladwell cites the ten-thousand-hour mark as being the amount of time it takes to be world-class in any field. In other words, it takes you around five years to acquire the confidence to consider yourself an expert.

However, while some of that skill and knowledge takes years to acquire, some of it may be low-hanging fruit. Either way, you've got to begin somewhere.

Every football Sunday we invite all our best friends and family to tailgate during the Philadelphia Eagles games. What we're learning is that we need to communicate with these people to make sure everybody brings enough beer and food. Over the past ten years, we learned through trial and error that the best approach is an email system.

The better we got at emailing, the more we wanted to engage everyone. So, instead of sending a static message, we learned how to create a .gif, which has resulted in endless entertainment for everyone since we tend to animate our friends doing dumb things.

Thus, not only have we mastered the art of figuring out how to never run out of cold beer, but we're building communication skills and graphic design knowledge that we can actively apply to our jobs.

It's one example of how you can use your Millennial efficiency to learn skills while also getting some benefit out of it, whether that's ensuring there's enough beer at the tailgate or mastering Prezi to create killer presentations for your department. Just because you're learning doesn't mean you can't have fun with it. Let your hair down and get creative.

FOCUS...FOCUS...FOCUS...

Between all the emailing, texting, IM-ing and phone calls, it's no wonder why our attention spans are so short. You're in the middle of something, and suddenly, your phone is ringing. Then, your computer starts dinging. Before you know it, two hours have gone by and you still haven't been able to finish a damn thing.

Having systems to keep yourself focused is important. Kate sets aside time to check email and times where she shuts it to get work done. Some people like to put their iPhones on silent and only check them at lunch. Others close all windows on their computers that they know will be distracting. Regardless, figure out a system that works best for you. Sure, Millennials can switch tasks more quickly, but multitasking is a myth. You should keep the temptation to try to multitask in check. Otherwise, you're all over the place, stressed out, making stupid mistakes, and getting little accomplished.

However, when you are figuring out your system, make sure it doesn't sacrifice the efficiency of the team. When you do, you'll get better at picking the right technology or putting into place more efficient processes because you'll understand how what you do today will impact where you are next year.

Keep in mind, though, that consistent doesn't mean perfect. It's about average speed, which is achieved by planning for failure so you know how to bounce back. If you need an assist, a great resource is part 2 of "The Ultimate Guide to Habits" from IWillTeachYouToBeRich. com called "Goal-Setting...the Right Way."

LEARN FROM OTHERS' MISTAKES

We've talked about evaluating in your first ninety days or resetting if you're a seasoned employee, but you can also learn a lot from the success and failure of other people. When you fail, you certainly should learn something. When your manager fails, use it as a guide to avoid the same pitfalls. As your career advances, you'll find yourself in the same situation he or she did.

Now, you don't want to go to somebody and say, "Hey, I know you failed on this. Could you tell me more about it?"

It will require some respectful questions directed toward the right people to find out exactly what happened, but those are the types of questions that pave the way for you to learn and grow.

Start with your close network and go from there. Maybe that includes a trusted peer or coworker or a past manager if you still maintain a good relationship. You don't want to be talking behind someone's back, but it's okay to ask pointed questions. Just avoid the temptation to trash-talk or gossip. Keep it professional and don't make it personal.

Also, observe how your coworkers and superiors interact with other people. If someone's communication with his or her colleague is a constant fail, pay attention to why that might be the case. Then, when it's your turn to interact with those people, you'll know what they respond to most positively.

TAKE TIME TO TAKE A STEP BACK

Reevaluate whom you're spending time with. Avoid expending too much energy with the Human Rain Delays of the world. You know whom we're talking about. They always have an excuse, and they always bring the room down. They're the kind of people that complain when it's too hot, and then they complain when it's too cold. They complain when it's Monday because the weekend is over, or they complain when it's Friday when a busy weekend is ahead.

There's always something.

Because they're not going to bring positive, productive energy to you, it's best that you try and avoid hanging out with them completely. Sometimes that's not possible if they're crawling all over your office.

In that case, make all attempts to respond to anything they say with positivity. Sometimes, it forces them to change the way they're framing a conversation or how they'll talk to you in the future.

Evaluate if your environment needs to change for you to continue to grow and improve.

Surely you've heard this quotation before: "If you're the smartest person in the room, you're in the wrong room." It speaks to surrounding yourself with people who are smarter than you, people to learn from. It's okay to be in those scenarios when you're helping elevate other people. However, make sure that even in your close circle of friends there are other people who are above your level of intelligence or work ethic whom you can productively and positively feed off of.

When you find yourself in the right room, go find the most talented person there and try to hang out with him or her. Learn from that person. Find a way to show him or her the value you bring as well. It's just as important as taking your seat at the table, which we discussed before. *Rhythm of Life* author Matthew Kelly says, "The people we surround ourselves with either raise or lower our standards. They either help us to become the best version of ourselves or encourage us to become lesser versions of ourselves. We become like our friends. No man becomes great on his own. No woman becomes great on her own. The people around them help to make them great. We all need people in our lives who raise our standards, remind us of our essential purpose, and challenge us to become the best version of ourselves."

This often requires a serious effort at evaluating whom you spend most of your time with. This is especially important for people in their early twenties. We're not saying to ditch everyone you went to college with, but make sure they are among those who bring out your best self. If you have an eye on becoming a senior vice president by the time you're thirty, and your best buds still want to get trashed at the bar four nights a week, it's time to reevaluate. You can keep them in your life, but make a real effort to expand your network to keep growing. When you start to have conversations with people who have different knowledge, skills, and talents, it keeps your mind open to new experiences and ideas.

Sometimes, you also should reevaluate your surroundings, too. In Rob's hometown, the running joke is that every decade one person makes it out.

If possible, go live somewhere else. Meet different people. Do what's uncomfortable. Walk into a bar where you don't know the bartender. Eat at a restaurant by yourself.

Being able to walk into any room and talk to whoever is there is practice for doing the same at the office. It goes back to some of the advice we've given about testing things and practicing them in low-pressure environments. That way, when the stakes are high, you come armed with experience and confidence.

RECOGNIZE WHEN IT'S YOU WHO'S BEING THE ASSHOLE

Look, we're not psychologists. If you can't look in the mirror and see where you might be wrong in any given situation, then maybe it's time you made an appointment with a shrink. Everyone screws up from time to time. True leadership stems from being able to admit it and grow from it.

Don't blame, make excuses, throw people under the bus, or point the finger. Be strong enough to look yourself in the mirror and get your shit together.

Often, hints about where you can improve is couched in frequent requests. If people are constantly verifying times with you before scheduling meetings, consider if you have a reputation for being late or not showing up.

On the flip side, don't sacrifice honesty in favor of not wanting to hurt someone's feelings. By putting yourself in their shoes, however, you can be honest without coming off as a heartless jerk. Don't sugarcoat, but don't go for the jugular, either.

HATE TECHNOLOGY? GET OVER IT BECAUSE IT'S HERE TO STAY

Technology is in everything. Our lights turn on and off with our phones, and we can send a photo in an instant to someone over in Japan. You should at least possess a hobby-level knowledge of technology to be able to function in today's digital world. You don't have to build your own computer, but having a basic understanding of how it works is critical to having a rudimentary understanding of the framework of society at this point.

HELP YOURSELF BY HELPING OTHERS

If you are comfortable with technology, it can further advance your knowledge to help people who aren't familiar with it. Maybe your parents don't know how to text, or Grandma is unfamiliar with surfing the internet. Their questions will provide insight into how they think and approach the digital world. It will also buy you tons of goodwill and give them peace of mind. Don't underestimate how valuable that can be.

In turn, you'll be able to be more productive and effective at advancing technology in the office because you can more easily anticipate what your coworkers might struggle with or fear.

When Kate had to introduce incognito browsing in Chrome to an older coworker to prevent date overwriting issues, she explained it by saying, "You really only use this if you're looking at porn." It broke the ice a little bit and made light of the situation, implying that of course her colleague had no previous use for that setting. Then they could move on to the actual, business-appropriate use for incognito.

Present information as a helpful tip that can save people time if they're interested. Without being condescending, offer to show them different options, and then let them decide which works best for them.

As a rule, tips for using Excel are among those that everyone is always receptive of.

DEVELOP AN ACHIEVABLE SYSTEM THAT WILL HELP YOU REACH YOUR GOALS

It takes a lot of energy to be creative, solve problems, and learn new things. Studies have proven that willpower and energy are limited resources. So, while it's true that you can develop and strengthen them, it's important to develop systems to help reduce the amount of willpower and energy you waste. Make it a habit, or a nonnegotiable, so you can just do it.

Here are some easy guidelines for developing an achievable one that will help you reach your goals:

1. SET ASIDE TIME EACH DAY FOR LEARNING OR READING.

It's fifteen minutes. It's half an hour. It could be when you wake up or when you go to bed. Reset your browser at the office to *The Skimm* or Google news, and spend five minutes getting caught up on what's going on in your industry and the world. Whatever way you slice it, make sure that at least once a day you're learning *something*.

2. GET TO WORK EARLIER.

Use that hour of quiet time to work on a project or get a head start on a daily report. If you're an hourly employee, set aside some time in the morning to create a plan of attack for the day ahead.

3. TURN OFF THE TV, PHONE, OR LAPTOP AN HOUR BEFORE BED.

Read a book instead to start getting your mind and body ready for a restful night of sleep. Keep paper on your nightstand for any last-minute thoughts you need to record.

4. RELY ON CHECKLISTS.

Whether it's a traditional day planner, Google calendar, or the notes app on your phone, use it to map out all the tasks you need to be doing today, tomorrow, this week, and so on. Check them off as they're completed to ensure nothing falls by the wayside. You'll feel a sense of accomplishment from checking things off your list. If you're like Kate, it will help you sleep better because you're not worrying about forgetting something.

Establishing and keeping a routine can sometimes be even more important than having a lot of time because it fosters a more productive environment. Just don't get stuck in a rut, no longer expanding your horizons or trying new things. It might be something as simple as driving to work one day and taking a bus the next. Sometimes, even something as simple as taking a different route will get your creative juices running.

LEARN HOW TO LEARN

Cosmetics maven Estee Lauder once said, "I didn't get to where I am by thinking about it or dreaming it. I got there by doing it."

Train your brain to look at everyone and everything as a learning opportunity.

Okay, how do I do that?

We thought you'd never ask!

1. ASK SOMEONE YOUNGER TO TEACH YOU SOMETHING.

Yeah, yeah, we get that we're all Digital Native geniuses, but there's always someone out there who knows more about something than you do. Even if you are familiar with the latest and greatest social media app, take a second look at it through a fresh perspective to learn a new angle. You'd be surprised at what you don't know.

2. SEEK ADVICE FROM THE EXPERTS.

Look to people for guidance in areas that are their strengths. Kate always involves interns with social media by involving them with the strategy. Sometimes they eventually take over the account; sometimes they don't. Either way, experts typically have a pulse on how to capitalize on something to ensure the highest ROI.

3. USE THE INTERNET.

Look for how-to videos on YouTube or Vimeo. Don't sit around and wait for someone to teach you how to edit a video or create a killer presentation using Prezi. Almost everything you need to know is available via online tutorials, which usually don't cost a thing.

4. TEACH OTHERS.

Don't hoard all that valuable knowledge like a frenzied squirrel. Share it! Teaching others is good practice for learning how to most effectively deal with different personality types and skill levels. Especially share those subtle skills that are hard to pick up via internet learning and that require practice with other humans, such as starting a conversation, negotiating, or public speaking.

BE A GO-GETTER, NOT A DO-NOTHING

When you're dealing with people who are less tech-savvy than you are, don't try to boil the ocean. As we talked about before, present the information in snack-sized pieces that they can chew, not choke on.

That applies to your own working knowledge of technology, too. Don't be intimidated by trying something new or letting yourself get frustrated when you don't immediately get it. Take advantage of those free online tutorials, and be patient, learning piece by piece.

Recently, Kate's company wanted to start producing video content. They had no budget for a video production team, though, and heard crickets when they asked if any of the employees wanted to take a shot.

Now, understand: Kate *hates* video content. When somebody puts a video on Facebook, she doesn't even watch it. So naturally, she avoided taking on the project as long as humanly possible until she had a thought. *You know what? This is totally out of my comfort zone, but it's still beneficial to learn. Even though I'm going to hate every minute of it, at least I'll be learning something new.*

Her company had a ton of video production and lighting equipment, but it was an ordeal to use.

Instead, she did some research and found a happy medium with the GoPro. After watching a few online tutorials to gain basic, working knowledge, she also taught herself how to edit the content and add sound and effects. It resulted in some lighter-weight videos that everyone loved and inspired another employee to take over the project.

Taking the initiative is always a good idea because, often, *someone* is watching. I don't mean they're watching in a creepy, Big Brother sort of way, but senior leaders will begin to take notice when you're producing something that everyone can benefit from. Thus, you'll become the go-to resource and almost cause a culture change simply by inviting an environment of fast learning.

Rob can trace a lot of his growth back to being more efficient and better at PowerPoint than other colleagues. People took notice that he could build a presentation better than most, and after a couple years he was put in charge of the entire company's budget presentation.

It certainly wasn't in his job description, but the CFO trusted his presentation skills enough to ask him to create something that would be presented to senior leaders and foreign investors.

The same thing happened to Kate. Although it's a pain in the ass, she always finds herself in charge of budgets because she's better than most at (and secretly loves) Excel. This is helpful to Kate because it provides her better visibility into the priorities of the entire department. Plus, if her boss can trust her with something as critical as the budget, he can trust her with a lot more.

Sometimes, it's not even skills that will land you these special roles to help accelerate your growth. It can be as simple as taking a complicated subject or business problem and making it very, very simple for others to understand. Once you are trusted with one thing, it opens the door for senior leaders to trust you with many more.

That's priceless.

CHAPTER 6 ACTION ITEMS

- ⏻ Learn something new. It doesn't have to be related to your job, but if it is, try deploying the PITCH method to get your company to pay for it.
- ⏻ Read (or listen to) a book.
- ⏻ Pick one day a week to do focused work. On that day, limit your distractions (email, texting, chat, social media) to predetermined chunks of time.

CHAPTER 7

....

SUSTAINING SUCCESS

....

HARD WORK DOESN'T end when you finally get to enjoy the sweet taste of success.

Just like anything worth pursuing, it requires a sustained effort. As we talked about in the last chapter, it can become easy to get comfortable and complacent when you settle into routine habits and systematic approaches to your work.

When that happens, you basically become an automated machine. Here's how to stay three-dimensional.

NEVER LET YOUR LIFE LOOK LIKE A RERUN

How much would you enjoy watching only one episode

of your favorite television show over and over and over?

You wouldn't. It would be boring, right?

Well, take that same approach to your career.

Even if you're killing it at your job right now, you still want to expand your involvement into things that could grow into future opportunities.

Through dozens of interviews with some of the most successful executives across multiple industries, a common thread was that the clear majority of them have outlets beyond their work that they're passionate about. It enables them to connect with people in different industries all over the world.

In doing so, they inevitably find more keys to open more doors. It keeps them creative, fresh. They know damn well that resting on their laurels will leave them falling flat.

If anyone ever shot us to the moon, we'd probably take a good look around and say, "Oh, wow, this is awesome. But Mars looks cool, too. We want to go there next."

That's how people become great at stuff. They hone their skills and know everything there is to know about the position they're in with an eye on advancing to the next level.

Yeah, but what if I do too many things and some fall off the map?

As card-carrying members of The Great Millennial Side Hustle, we've both pursued outside projects to bring us additional income. Sometimes those endeavors work out; sometimes they don't. However, each one has given us a better perspective in life. We've always learned *something* in the process.

In the *Quartz* article "Millennials Are Obsessed with Side Hustles Because They're All We've Got," writer Catherine Baab-Muguira nailed it when she said, "Millennials didn't invent the second job. They just branded it."

Rob was a coach in grad school, and in his mind, it's something he'd like to do again when he retires. He keeps a foot inside that world by maintaining and making new contacts to increase the likelihood that he can get right back into coaching when the time is right.

Uh, okay. But I still don't know what to do...

Take the first step!

That's how people end up kicking ass, whether it's disrupting an industry or blowing through gender stereotypes. They start. Anywhere. Anyhow. They don't care if the conditions are perfect, or if they're being slighted. Once they get started, all they need is momentum to make it work.

The first time Amelia Earhart was asked to fly around the world, she was told that some guy would be paid to supervise her. Even crazier? She *wasn't* getting paid.

Do you know what she said?

"Okay, whatevs. Tell him to hurry his ass up and get in this flying tin can because I've got places to go."

We're paraphrasing from the *Upstart Business Journal*'s article "Why Amelia Earhart's 1925 Gamble Should Inspire Entrepreneurs," but the point is she decided that starting somewhere under less than favorable conditions was better than not starting at all. There was no sitting around whining or complaining, dreaming of the day when the ideal situation would come her way. She knew that if she could just get the ball rolling, people would catch on, the momentum would take hold, and both would accelerate her toward her goal of flying solo.

The same author of that article, Ryan Holiday, also wrote

the book *The Obstacle Is the Way*. In it, he says, "For a lot of reasons, it's never been easier to start a company, publish a book, or create your own personal brand. Legally, it's easier. Technically, it's easier, but even with these barriers, people still delay. They're waiting for the right conditions, right opportunity, or they're testing the waters, researching it."

Sit around and wait for something to fall into your lap? To hell with that. Make your **own** luck.

It's one of the reasons we decided to write this book. We thought to ourselves, *"Let's sign up for this, and that way, we have money invested and deadlines to meet."* We knew the process wouldn't be perfect, but we had to start somewhere.

You should have seen our files for this book. They were covered in red markings and placeholders for a story that Rob had or a quotation Kate remembered from an interview we conducted. There were endless lists and Google docs that were constantly being updated, revised, or scrapped.

SUCCESS DOESN'T BRING HAPPINESS— HAPPINESS BRINGS SUCCESS

Blah, blah, blah, you're probably thinking. Seriously

though; this isn't just some inspirational quotation to pin to your Pinterest board. Shawn Achor, author of *The Happiness Advantage*, paraphrases a study: "If we know the intelligence and technical skills of an employee, we can actually only predict about 25% of the job success. 75% of long-term job success is predicted not by intelligence and technical skills, which is normally how we hire, educate and train, but it's predicted by three other umbrella categories. It's optimism (which is the belief that your behavior matters in the midst of challenge), your social connection (whether or not you have depth and breadth in social relationships) and the way you perceive stress."

Everything he talks about reinforces why it's so important to develop achievable systems, find a seat at the table, and surround yourself with people who are smarter than you are. Each helps to build confidence, which in turn encourages a happier mind-set and paves the way to success.

BECOME A MENTOR

Mentoring is a good way to diversify your development. Regardless of whether those you mentor are older than you or younger, sometime in the future they might be able to help you.

We try to stay in touch with all the people we've ever mentored. In fact, we reached out to a lot of them as we were writing this book. Had we not fostered those relationships, we might have missed an opportunity to get their valuable input.

Focus on growing anyone who is lower on the corporate ladder than you are. It's not only helpful for your success, but it will show your bosses, senior leaders, and coworkers your ability to develop the individual to ensure a better team.

VOLUNTEER

As we mentioned in chapter 5, Kate's friend Cady does a lot of pro-bono consulting or, as she calls it, "Skillanthropy." It makes her feel good and builds her confidence, but it also has the potential to turn into future career opportunities—especially if she ever wants to pursue consulting full-time.

We Millennials respond particularly well to the positive effects of volunteering because we are able to see that we're making a difference in real time. If we volunteer to clean up a park, we can immediately see and appreciate the "before and after." Not to mention, we're taking charge with being environmentally responsible.

Volunteering is such a win-win. You find something that you care about, and you're able to feel as if you're making a difference while at the same time expanding your network.

Pick a charity that you believe in, and support their efforts either financially or with your time and talents. One of our favorites is the Tara Miller Melanoma Foundation, which was started by our friend Tara, a Millennial herself, before she passed away from cancer at age twenty-nine. The three things we like best about the foundation are these:

1. 100% of money raised goes directly toward research.

2. The Miller family provides ongoing transparency into the research that is being funded and the progress being made.

3. Tara's ambition to start the foundation while battling stage-four brain cancer inspired a diverse group of people to bring their talents and resources together to make an impact.

There are people we've met working for this foundation that we wouldn't have met otherwise. Some of them just became great friends. That's valuable. Maybe further down the road these people could be allies in different parts of life or bring about new opportunities. However, the amazing thing about volunteering is you already did something meaningful.

Pick something you feel passionate about, and take a hands-on approach.

Or, if you're lazy and just want to send a check to the Tara Miller Melanoma Foundation, please feel free to do so. One hundred percent of the proceeds will go to cancer research.

NETWORK

Get out of the house. Seriously. Turn off the Netflix and go.

Remember our friend Gretchen from chapter 1? If you make an effort to drag your ass off the couch and go to a party, you might end up with a new job.

No matter where you are or what you are doing, greet people with a positive attitude, and you'll always have a warm opener. You won't have to worry about what to talk about, because you've been reading *The Skimm* and other news aggregates to ensure you won't be stuck having the same boring conversation about the weather.

Because of that, chances are much better that people will remember you and the meaningful conversation you shared.

INVEST

Earlier in the book, we covered why it's important to invest and get your finances in order so that you can ensure that both your current and future needs are going to be met.

It's hard to sustain any success on the job when you're too preoccupied stressing over how you're going to scrape enough money together to make your car payment.

The number-one tip that Felice, the financial planner we mentioned earlier, has for Millennials is to get serious about saving and take planning for the future seriously. She says it's tougher for our generation in particular to do, because we've typically had more to start with. Few of us save the bacon grease to cook in the next day. Ahem, you with the student loans who insists on eating out seven days a week: you can use this shit to make everything you cook taste better.

If your company offers a 401(k) match, take advantage of it! That's free money. Get out of credit card debt ASAP. You shouldn't be taking on high-interest debt that compounds and digs you into a deeper hole. If you don't understand debt, interest rates, or investment options at a basic level, put down this book and go learn more about it. Our blog, MillennialReboot.com, is a great place to start, as is IWill-TeachYouToBeRich.com.

It goes back to willpower being a muscle you need to exercise. Make sure that you're spending within your means and you're saving. Life is going to throw you a curve ball from time to time, and you've got to be able to cover your ass when it does.

Do everything you can today to propel you to a better tomorrow.

PUTTING THE BALL IN MOTION

Start.

We're emphasizing the period on this one. Notice that it's not a comma or ellipsis following that word.

To be effective at anything, you must take a step forward, However, it's also going to require time and actual commitment.

When you get a small win by doing one thing, it incentivizes you to start doing more. If you pay off one credit card, then you can say, "Okay, great. Now I can pay off a chunk of the next credit card."

Set actionable, achievable goals to start building your confidence. Then, take advantage of the momentum.

A lot of times, we Digital Natives struggle with considering time spent as time *well* spent. We feel that if we're just thinking and not doing, we're not accomplishing anything.

It's important to take a step back to think about what your priorities are now and what they will be in the future. It's the basis for how you can identify what you should add or take off your plate to better equip yourself to meet those goals.

Remember that thinking is hard work and takes time, so you should plan time for it. People used to naturally have more time to think because they had nothing to do as they sat in waiting rooms, waited for the bus, waited for friends to show up to dinner, and so on. They had plenty of time to think while they were "just waiting." Now we have smartphones, so we can literally fill every minute with doing something—productive or not.

You may be lucky enough to work for a company that actively encourages employees to dedicate a percentage of their work week to side projects. Even if you don't, though, be proactive and allocate some of your own time. We don't suggest using your entire weekend or every evening in the pursuit of self-evaluation, but you can find a healthy balance.

Maybe it's just spending an hour doing pro-bono consulting every Tuesday night or joining a recreational softball team. Figure out what your time allows, even if you feel as if you have none to spare.

Plus, if you don't have any time, it's a clear indication that

now is the time to figure out what to cut and rearrange to make time for growth. You don't want to spread yourself so thin that you're a master of nothing.

Make it a priority to reevaluate every six months to determine if you're on the right track.

SAY YES!

Sometimes it seems as if the older we get, the more the word *no* begins to invade our vocabulary.

According to Ramit Sethi, the *New York Times* best-selling author of *I Will Teach You to Be Rich*, "When we're confronted with a new opportunity, our mind naturally offers all kinds of reasons to say no. Kite surfing? No. New karaoke place down the street? No. Hanging out with a group of new people? No... It's much easier to do what we already know, and most of the time, that's okay. If you don't like the dance, that's fine. If you're not careful, though, suddenly, you're waking up, going to work, coming home. Same friends, same TV shows, same everything, every week. By default, life turns us into a routine, but every once in a while, something new comes along. If you notice, you can sense your gut reaction gearing up to say no. In that very small split second, if you pause and make the decision to live a different kind of life, a life where you say yes to special opportunities, you can reap amazing, extraordinary rewards. What's the last special opportunity you got? Maybe it's getting invited to a friend's birthday party where you meet your future husband or wife."

We get it. Sometimes it's uncomfortable to go out. It takes a lot of energy to meet and engage new people, but you've got to dig deep and just go with it. You never know what you could be missing.

SEND THE ELEVATOR BACK DOWN

Kevin Spacey once said, "If you've done well, it's your obligation to spend a good portion of your time sending the elevator back down."

Success doesn't come easy, but when you manage to make your dreams a reality through a combination of hard work and implementing the skills you've learned over the past few chapters, make sure you're always quick to open doors for others.

Doing so won't discount the blood, sweat, and tears you've put into getting to where you are today. However, somewhere along that journey, someone threw you a bone; that person believed in you when you felt unsure and talked you down from the ledge during tough times.

Return the favor by paying it forward.

CHAPTER 7 ACTION ITEMS

- ⏻ Do a health check on your finances. Prioritize paying off credit card debt and then investing in your future
- ⏻ Commit to a new social activity and set a minimum time to stick with it. Join a book (or wine) club, attend a weekly workout class, or sign up for pottery lessons. Build relationships beyond your typical circle of friends and coworkers.
- ⏻ Consider whom you can help. Volunteer for a charity or join a mentor program.

CONCLUSION

AT THIS POINT in the game, we hope you're better able to see that all those issues between old-school and new-school mentalities in business aren't because of a generational gap. They're because of a **communication** gap.

Both groups can learn from each other and must be able to appreciate what each brings to the table.

The next steps are on you: Show up, ask questions, schedule meaningful check-ins with your manager, answer expeditiously, and most importantly, do the things you say you're going to do.

Remember, you must do more than just sit back and complain about everything that pisses you off at work. Be proactive, get off your ass, and do something about it.

You're armed with even more superpowers now than you were when you first picked up this book. You've acquired the right knowledge base, you understand the basic leadership styles of people you'll run into at work, and more importantly, you know how to navigate some pretty choppy waters with confidence and finesse.

Success isn't going to come by binge-watching television or blowing off work because you had too many Fireball shots last night. Your job is to be the best damn employee your company ever had—to be innovative, always eager to learn, and one who plays well with others, actively pays it forward, goes above and beyond, and encourages inclusiveness to further the team, not just yourself.

Keep reminding yourself, ***don't be a dick***—no matter what the situation or who you're dealing with. Sustaining your success is done by actively advancing yourself both personally and professionally.

Flip back through these pages when you need a quick refresher, or hit up our blog, MillennialReboot.com, for updated resources and best practices being utilized by high performing professionals around the world.

You've got what it takes to shatter the preconceived notions that the corporate world has about Millennials. Lead the charge and enjoy the journey that will lead you away from your cubicle and into the corner office.

ADDITIONAL RESOURCES

⏻ Our Blog: MillennialReboot.com

PRODUCTIVITY

⏻ News: TheSkimm.com

⏻ Audio Books: Audible.com

⏻ Email Unsubscribe Service: Unroll.me

⏻ Waterproof Notepad: MyAquaNotes.com

⏻ How to Do Almost Anything: YouTube.com

PERSONAL FINANCE AND INCOME BUILDING

⏻ Ramit Sethi's IWillTeachYouToBeRich.com

SKILLANTHROPY

⏻ Taproot: TaprootFoundation.org

⏻ Catch a Fire: CatchAFire.org

CHARITIES

⏻ Tara Miller Melanoma Foundation: TaraMillerFoundation.org

OTHER BOOKS WE RECOMMEND

⏻ *Adulting: How to Become a Grown-Up in 468 Easy(ish) Steps* by Kelly Williams Brown

⏻ *Brief: Make a Bigger Impact by Saying Less* by Joseph McCormack

⏻ *Freakonomics: A Rogue Economist Explores the Hidden Side of Everything* by Stephen J. Dubner and Steven Levitt

⏻ *How to Fail at Almost Everything and Still Win Big: Kind of the Story of My Life* by Scott Adams

⏻ *How to Win Friends and Influence People* by Dale Carnegie

⏻ *Know Your Value* by Mika Brzezinski

⏻ *Lean In* by Sheryl Sandberg

⏻ *Nice Girls Don't Get the Corner Office: Unconscious Mistakes Women Make That Sabotage Their Careers* by Lois P. Frankel

⏻ *Perfecting Your Pitch: How to Succeed in Business and in Life by Finding Words That Work* by Ronald M. Shapiro with Jeff Barker

⏻ *The Power of Habit: Why We Do What We Do in Life and Business* by Charles Duhigg

⏻ *Steal Like an Artist: 10 Things Nobody Told You About Being Creative* by Austin Kleon

⏻ *The Tipping Point: How Little Things Can Make a Big Difference* and *Blink: The Power of Thinking Without Thinking* by Malcolm Gladwell

ACKNOWLEDGMENTS

FOR THE FOUNDATION and encouragement to maximize our potential, we'd like to acknowledge Kate's parents, Anne and Chris, and her sister, Jackie; Rob's mother, Annette; the professors that made us uncomfortable and exposed us to real work scenarios; the rowing coaches that taught us about so much more than just sports; the City of Philadelphia and PennAC Rowing Association where we first met; our friends who are still our friends after we disappeared for a summer to write this book, the ones who gave input and stories for the book, and the ones that let us crash at their shore house when we needed a change of scenery.

Also, for specifically helping with this book, we'd like to thank Kelsey Capps, KC Cox, Grace Doepker, Dan Gallagher, Felice Hubbard, the Internet for putting so much information at our fingertips, Ashley LaBau, Lindsey Masciangelo, Jake Miller, Katie Mitchell, Vicki Neidigh, Alex Richmond, Cindy Stutman, Neil Sullivan, Amy Wells and Sam Wood.

ABOUT THE AUTHORS

KATE ATHMER and ROB JOHNSON are Millennial MBAs with a drive to help the go-getters of their generation overcome traditional negative Millennial stereotypes and lead corporate America through the technology revolution.

Kate runs demand marketing for a software startup, advocating regularly for technology to enable advanced strategies. As a cofounder of GreenLit Consulting, she also provides career and brand advice for peers, recent graduates, and anyone looking to advance. A graduate of the University of Dayton with an MBA from the University of Tennessee, Kate credits a combination of strong mentors, diverse educational and athletic opportunities, tenacity, and strategic content consumption for her success in the workplace.

Rob has experience as a sports and entertainment executive, collegiate rowing coach, and adjunct professor. He is driven by creativity and innovation, which he puts to practice as a cofounder of GreenLit Consulting. Rob has grown his career in part by bridging the technology divide and committing to the professional development of others. After graduating from Marietta College, Rob began his professional career in the NFL as the marketing coordinator for the Jacksonville Jaguars. While in Jacksonville, he earned his MBA from the Davis College of Business at Jacksonville University.

Both Kate and Rob reside in Center City, Philadelphia.

Made in the USA
Lexington, KY
10 December 2016